July 2007
A gift from Marilen Abesamis ...

Joey Velasco *"Hapag ng Pag-asa"* (Table of Hope), 2005 Oil on Canvas 48 x 96 in

+

AMDG

Our Lady Mary Mediatrix of All Grace, intercede for us.

THEY HAVE JESUS

The Stories of the Children of Hapag

by

Joey A. Velasco

Published by Kenosis Publications

Editor: Ilsa Belmonte Reyes
Cover Design: Joey Velasco and Demetrio DelaCruz
Layout design: Joey Velasco
Paintings and Illustrations: Joey Velasco

Printed 2006
2nd Printing 2007

ISBN 978-971-93658-0-8

Set in 12 pt Adobe Garamond Pro
Printed in the Philippines by LCD Press Commercial Inc.

To my wife, Queeny
and to my children
Marco, Chiara, Clarisse, and Marti
with whom I play war games
under the rain...

TABLE OF CONTENTS

The Roman Catholic Archbishop of Manila
121 Arzobispo Street, Intramuros
P.O. Box 132
Manila, Philippines

Foreword

A dinner table reveals a lot about hunger, manners and relations. Who sits near the host, who serves the guest or who cares for the youngest, all these are made known at the family dinner.

More than taste, meanings are associated with what one eats or even on how one sits at the table. Friendship, old ties or the loss of it are suddenly recalled when diners meet, and the passing of food is enriched with stories and sharing of familiar knowledge and feelings.

Surprisingly some meals are taken hurriedly, thus crumbs fly and the meaning of the coming together is lost.

In the Israelites' flight to safety at the night of the great escape (Exodus) the surprise of running away left the people with many experiences unexplained; symbols were lost, as people fled in fright. Thus many more meals will be celebrated in order to get to the meaning of their paschal meal. And "one of your children will ask you, what does this ritual mean?"

Tell us that some meals have become so private and solitary that no one asks a question? What do we eat? Where's the *patis*? Who's coming to dinner? The art of conversation and telling stories has already been lost at many dining tables. More than enjoying a repast, a diner has need to reveal other wants.

Every child diner at the *hapag* reveals a story of more hunger than a plate of rice could satisfy. Onse, a nine year old lad, for example sits at the *hapag ng pag-asa*, his plate cleaned to the last crumb, but he listens still to feed his other hungers as a cart-pushing scavenger whose father is a drug addict and the mama is a club strip dancer.

At the table of the Master, Itok, the eleven-year old bread winner, another cart pushing scavenger, whispers that he has gone number of times to jail after having been caught in a number of thieveries. What hunger and desires did this talented scavenger bring to the feet of Jesus and those who believe in Jesus? A Christian community is fittingly disturbed as it watches the masqueraded struggle between good and evil, between wealth and poverty, between greed and compassion, power and weakness as played in the lives of these children robbed of innocence and security of an ordinary growing youth.

Around the table were young people, including one whose hurt dug deep into her heart and completely erased whatever dignity a young girl had. Much misery is hidden behind the faces of the hapag children whose lives are further shrouded in the destitution of cemetery shack-dwellers and pushcart lodgers.

Is the *hapag* still waiting for food, or are the poor young diners announcing a different hunger that makes young and old, rich and poor, the educated and the ignorant equally famished for nourishment that only love could satisfy?

The artist Joey Velasco's portrait of the young asks us more questions about ourselves rather than probe the *hapag* children. Rather than ask "why" these young people live in such an unkind and violent world, the challenge to the beholder of the portrait should be "how" in a Christian community the poor children could be helped out of such misery.

Pope Benedict XVI in his first encyclical letter, DEUS CARITAS EST, reminded us that the essential core of communion, at the heart of love, remains the same: "within the community of believers there can never be room for a poverty that denies anyone what is needed for a dignified life". (DCE, 20).

The *hapag* is not an accusatory portrait. But the reality of the shacks under the bridges and the tunnels of homes along esteros, or the slums among the tombs from which many more young ones come, challenges every believer in the Christ who loves the poor. "How" can we be Christians to them? Can a good Christian, a true lover of Jesus, be without compassion for the poor?

Welcome this portrait into your own and make the dining table serving life not just a table of hope, but **isang HAPAG-IBIG or hapag ng pag-ibig.**[*]

+ **GAUDENCIO B. CARDINAL ROSALES**
Archbishop of Manila
Pondo ng Pinoy

---

[*] Table of Love

Foreword

I first saw a replica of the *Hapag* painting in a billboard along Edsa near the Guadalupe bridge. The faces and appearances of the children in the painting all look too familiar. I see them everywhere. They march in and out of our consciousness without evoking emotions of pity or disgust. They are simply part of the landscape, their numbers growing everyday. Poverty stares at us in every corner of the land daily that we no longer see it.

But this particular painting disturbed and excited me.

Jesus sharing a meal with starving children reminiscent of the last supper in the affluent district of Makati. Was it the setting that was upsetting? Was it telling me that I have forgotten Jesus because I have allowed these children to go wayward and hungry? Has shallow piety replaced genuine caring for the poor? Has charity not gone beyond pity towards a search for authentic expressions of Christian stewardship?

Have we simply accepted our fate that we are a country of beggars because there is Jesus who will love them even if I don't... because I am too busy to care?

Am I disturbed because I still see myself in one of them? I may have an education and the opportunity to provide my children a better quality of life than I had as a child, but I still feel poor because many others are starving and living in miserable conditions around me.

On the other hand, the picture excites me. In the midst of a bleak scenario, Jesus is there. His light shines. His love overflows. Coming from the poor, I thought it was the blessing of a good education that was my passport to a better life. But it was not enough. It

in fact made me ambitious and selfish that I forgot where I came from and the many who were left behind. I only found hope and the fullness of life when I found Jesus.

The reality of Jesus' love is moving many of us to bring this country from darkness to light, from despair to hope… to rise above division and conflict, to be one people in our journey to our promised land.

I am excited to see my children raise their family in a squatter-free, slum-free country. I am excited to see a new generation of healthy and bright children who will no longer beg in the streets or scavenge food from garbage.

I am excited to see the healthy and happy faces of the children in the next Hapag painting of Joey Velasco.

Tony Meloto
Gawad Kalinga Worker
Ramon Magsaysay Awardee 2006

"A painting has inspired this book
and the faces of poverty inspired the painting
but it was faith that inspired the artist.

The artist-turned-writer now hopes that
The Spirit who inspired him to see in faith
will now inspire us to act with love."

Fr. Francis O. Gustilo, SDB

INTRODUCTION

I have painted with my hand and I have also painted with my heart.

To hand-paint means to be faithful to the principles of colors, tones, strokes, lights and shadows. Oftentimes, the work can spring from fragments of styles and techniques one culls from influences absorbed from the Great Masters. It can be rendered in many forms like figure art, landscape, seascape, still life, floral, etc. It is expressed in different approaches of realism, surrealism, impressionism, expressionism, cubism and abstract. It is a synergy between hand and brush. The artist can be detached from his work. It is a work of objectivity. In aesthetic terms, he defines his Art.

On the other hand, to heart-paint means more than all that. It means seeing some elements undetected by the naked eye. The heart-painter does not just look at his painting, but his painting looks at him and speaks to him on different levels. His art defines him. It is not deliberate. It happens spontaneously. It is a synergy between the heart and what is beyond the canvas. He does not paint something that he does not believe in or something detached from his life. He is fearless. He deals not just with concepts and ideas. He dabs his brush with truth. He smudges the paint because his life has been touched by what he has seen or by what has been done to him. It is an "all-absorbing" process. To heart-paint is also to bear witness to what he paints. One vouchsafes by one's experience what he paints. It is painting in a deeper way.

It happened to me last year when I painted the *Hapag ng Pag-asa* (The Table of Hope). Pictorially, the painting suggested a spiritual maelstrom, with the viewer caught between tensions of forces: tur moil and stillness. The work emitted a field of energy, a halation of light, suggesting transcendence. It was so amazing how the public accepted it and how it has whipped up a whirlpool of emotions from people whose lives were touched by it. Indeed, the *Hapag* called its viewer to action. "What can I do to help and share?" was the oft-repeated question every time a person looked at the faces of the characters. It was an unforgettable experience. I felt so much joy because it had the appeal of sending a rich message.

Other questions that unfailingly get to be asked are: "Who are these kids?" "Where are they from?" "Do you know them?" "Were they just products of your imagination?" Honestly, I did not have a chance to personally know them. I just got these kids from different areas in Quezon City, gave them food, and gathered them to pose for me. I have always used references whenever I would paint. Usually, I take several pictures and select the best before I start. I set up the lighting myself and use a lot of effects and props galore. In the case of *Hapag,* the children went back to their harsh and cruel life. Dining with Christ at the table of hope became just digital and not real during the initial stage of my project.

Pressing the shutter of my camera became, so to speak, an escape route from genuinely loving and serving the poor as Christ did. Yes, the picture was painted on a canvas and has touched hearts, but I felt I exploited the children because I did not even at least desire to know them and offer a fraction of the charity that was portrayed in my work. I did not bother to ask about their lives and their exigencies. This became so clear when I finished the work and felt consumed by it. I sat on my chair and realized I was not really generous enough. Months had passed and the painting became the topic of both homilies and art discussions. I strongly felt that it had already taken on a life of its own.

Every morning, as early as five, I would sit at our dining table and look at the huge painting looking down at me as though it were painted by someone else. It began to speak back to me. I could not believe that my hand and heart were used by a higher force to depict God's love. Then, I began to wonder what had happened to these unknown and unnamed subjects/models...where they are now...what they are doing...or if they are still alive. Whenever I look at their faces, I would see myself in each of them. They are me, actually... at different stages of my life. They would speak to me...and I would listen very carefully. It was haunting.

Suddenly, I found myself looking at a painting which looked at me through windows provided by a mere canvas. I have uncovered some truths and I have bared something that I felt had to be dealt with. Their frail voices resonated within me and they whimpered in this quagmire I have fallen into. I realized that it was I who was experiencing a certain hunger and I was eager to have my place in that table of hope. I felt so restless.

After a year since I finished the *Hapag*, I found myself digging at the almost crumpled and oil paint-stained reference photo prints, some torn apart because of the adhesive tape that was removed from them. I needed them as guide for identification when I asked around, especially in the outskirts of the asphalt jungle. Searching for each single kid of *Hapag* was not some sort of an enjoyable thrill adventure. It was like spiraling into Dante's Inferno. Before I even got onto the roads leading to their territories, I was assaulted by the unbelievable stench and filth that filled the labyrinthine streets. Tattooed men, who were drinking gin in broad day light, stared at me suspiciously, like a pack of hyenas whose eyes knew the darkness in my soul. I went as far as North Cemetery, La Dakila, Litex, Yuen, Lilac, Karangalan, and Fairlaine under the bridge. It was a long and rough journey.

Poverty and misery have indeed ravaged our people tremendously. "Truth is stranger than fiction," so they say. Every child I successfully found was like a treasure rediscovered. They still knew me and were surprised to see me again. "Does this mean free noodles again?" their eyes asked with excitement. It was the time to make up for the lost opportunities of not having had exerted the effort to know them earlier. I spent time with them and I even tried touching their wounds. By crossing the line from a mere bystander to a real friend, I was beginning to know gradually who the *"batang-hapags"* were.

Their situation was inconceivable but I knew it was just a speck in comparison to the massive poverty that has marred our nation. Children treated as mosquitoes and stray cats, never-ending suffering, squalid living, broken lives and unfulfilled dreams... the causes of this misery are not only neglect, indolence and lack of opportunities, but the opportunism, fueled by greed, of the privileged few. To make matters worse, this greed has been glorified by society and media in the guise of competition, and it has calcified into all facets of society that it has produced more and more poor people. My blood boils at the mere thought and sight of it. It is definitely not God's will. This situation is an abomination before the face of God who created the world for all to enjoy.

I do not aim to do a Mother Theresa here or to fire up a grand vision like that of the great Tony Meloto whose environmental and social reengineering of Gawad Kalinga* is becoming global. I am e that I am surely not a powerful force to advocate change that will

---

*   **Gawad Kalinga** is a Philippine-based movement that envisions building 700,000 homes in 7000 communities in 7 years. It was formally launched on October 4, 2003 with October 4, 2010 as the target date for delivery. Gawad Kalinga (GK) , translated in English means "to give care," and it is an alternative solution to the blatant problem of poverty not just in the Philippines but the world. Its approach is integrated, holistic and sustainable – a concrete action plan to rebuild this nation by harnessing the best of the Filipino – our faith and our patriotism.

prevent hunger and raise funds. I am not a wealthy person. I cannot be a front-liner of any movement. But I know I can make a difference. This is my personal healing and transformative journey through the children's pain, hope, faith, and liberation that can reach other generations and cultures.

Countless books have been written in the past about the triumph of the human spirit and about great men who were larger than life. This simple book purports to share the stories of a handful of small lives whose voices are often unheard and whose tiny dreams are shattered before they can even take form. I just allowed them to speak for themselves even amidst the environment of cynicism. Their stories do not seem much because they are so simple, but they are definitely deep because they articulate and mirror the ills of society.

I am writing this book not out of conceit or in order to highlight the rare privilege of having painted with and from the heart. I am not sharing my strength as an artist or as a writer, but my weakness as a fellow journeyer who witnessed these children drifting in the dark. Initially, I thought they were lost only to find out in the end that I was the one who was actually lost. It is not a testimony of how I pitied poor children. It is an acknowledgement of God's abounding compassion on me. I am writing this to share how the Lord Himself painted through me and continues to reveal His message of hope and unconditional love through my humble work. In doing this, I wish to commit myself more and to live up to what is yet to unfold in the pages of this book.

Joey A. Velasco 2006
http://www.joeyvelasco.com
hapagpainting@yahoo.com

PREFACE

These are stories of real people.

After a year since I photographed these kids, I searched for each one of them in the outskirts of their respective areas and learned about their life stories. I was able to gather tons of pictures, a mini DV, and six cassette tapes of recorded interviews which my assistant transcribed on the computer: the life of Nene in the cemetery; the bruises and bondage of Itok; the simplicity and the warmth of Emong; the faith of the family of Jun and Roselle; the humbling experiences of Onse; the havoc of Tinay; the Sudan child's hunger; the powerlessness of Dodoy; the far gaze of Buknoy; the scarred life of Joyce; the wounds of Michael; and the friend in Jesus. The stories are not to be read with a full stomach.

I did not hesitate to narrate all the stories, even the harsh and sordid ones. At least three of them were sexually abused and many of them were physically maltreated. I am aware that this would be painful to some and threatening to a few readers. I knew they were sensitive issues, but found it best to be truthful and not to delete them. It happens in many areas of our society and it is but a tip of a hovering mountain of muck. These children symbolize and represent a bigger and more general reality today.

These are real stories of real people.

I am morally obligated, however, to protect the privacy and confidentiality of these characters. To prevent them from being marked especially in their growing years, I refrained from using their real names and I opted to pixelate their photos sacrificing the realism of the shots. It would be rude and would curtail their privacy if I unveil them in this medium. Besides, it would aggravate the injustices they are now facing so tremendously. Moreover, I changed the specific names of some places to conceal the children all the more and treat this subject so carefully. This is preferably meant for adult reading.

This book is not meant to be read from cover to cover. It is suggested that it is read separately per chapter as each individual story is independent from each other. The book may be started from the middle or from the end.

I have filled the book with stories because I believe it is the best way to comprehend *Hapag*. These stories are not rare stories. There are millions of children like them in the different corners of our society. I only hope they become springboards for your own stories as what they did to my own life story.

THEY HAVE JESUS

THEY HAVE JESUS

CHAPTER 1

The Niche of Nené

S trangely, the snatcher Judas-looking kid* at the extreme
left of the *Hapag* painting was not a boy but a girl. Yes, I
chanced upon this ten-year-old girl during the funeral of my
Uncle Rudy at the century-old Manila North Cemetery in
April 2005.

My eyes could not believe what I saw in that huge 54-hect-
are cemetery which was once upon a time the final resting place of
illustrious Filipinos like Sergio Osmeña, Manuel Roxas and Ramon

---

* **Judas** refers just to what she portrayed in the painting and not as a betrayer in real life.

Magsaysay and other great figures of our country. Thousands of squatters use the mausoleums as surreal homes where bones are swept out of crypts to make room for their makeshift furniture. They have practically lived in that cemetery among the gravestones of the dead for generations and they have already established a community or barangay in that shantytown. I had goose bumps. How ironic. The place which was supposedly for the dead was the place where people lived in order to survive. Some people die long before their actual physical death...

After the niche of my uncle was sealed and the epitaph was mounted, the bereaved family distributed some biscuits and fruit juices in tetra packs to the cemetery dwellers who were curiously watching our ceremonial rites. Like black piranhas, they attacked the food as though there were no tomorrow. There was stampede and pandemonium enough to shake the dead underneath the ground.

What caught my attention was a short-haired little girl carrying her one-year-old brother from a distance. She could not join the crowd no matter how much she wanted to because she was carrying her baby brother and she could not leave their *kariton* (pushcart) because everything would most surely be looted the minute she left it. She was pensive as shown by her crumpled forehead. She looked pathetic and hungry. She had that far-away look as if fearful of the challenges of tomorrow.

I stole a shot.

I did not know where to use that photo at that time. I first thought of using it for my GSIS** art competition entry because it had a social statement appeal. But the theme of the contest turned out to be *"Fiesta at Kasinayan"* so I just filed it in my drawer for future use. Not long after, I began working on my *Hapag ng Pag-asa* (Table of Hope). I gathered the participants from different places, but that boyish-looking girl's face continued to boggle my mind. In my painting, I wanted to portray her as a child who was forced by adults or by circumstances to steal in order to survive. I needed a face that looked so anxious and frightened because she was being hounded by the syndicate that prompted her to do the crime. She was in that gathering not for the meal but in order to tell Jesus of her predicament. She had indeed the perfect expression to portray a child thief.

My need to look for her was like her hunger for food. She was the first disciple I sought. I packed my digital camera, video camera and tape recorder and hit the road at exactly 10a.m. I found myself traversing that stretch of oily cholesterol road called *"La Loma"* where

** Government Service Insurance System in the Philippines

5

there was a long array of crunchy red-hot lechons modernly skewered with sturdy cylindrical poles. Perpendicular to that street was the huge entrance gate of Manila North Cemetery. Where was little Judas? My van glided through and made a slow turn towards the road that lead to my Tito Rudy's grave. I was anxiously looking to my left and to my right in the hope that I could catch the 'wanted' kid and hitch a ride on her kariton. Once again, I saw the shanties of the living whose number might even be more than the dead. They wasted their lives hanging around on street corners drinking cheap booze and sniffing toxic glue. They seemed lazier than the corpses and skeletons around. I was crazily imagining throwing one whole lechon at them and spraying it with Mang Tomas Sauce using a fire hose. They would definitely kill each other and devour the pig like vultures of the southwestern forest of Ethiopia. How cruel of me to have entertained such a thought!

It was impossible for me alone to find that little Judas amidst the 5,000 or so "Golgothic settlers." I requested Aling Chato, the caretaker of my uncle's abode, to assist me at this stage. I slipped the crumpled picture into her hand together with a one hundred peso bill. After waiting for thirty minutes, they finally arrived.

Lo and behold! Aling Chato shackled Little Judas in her hand like "Kunta Kinte"**** as they appeared from the heaps of dusty marble tombs. She was no longer the short-haired boyish girl I saw a year ago. Her hair was so long, unkempt and sticky. Her clothes were tattered and smelly. Her bare feet were soiled with mud and grease. She looked like the Count of Monte Cristo shortly after escaping from Chateau d'If. I did not recognize her at all.

***   Kunta Kinte was the enslaved African character of the novel Roots by Alex Haley.

I only knew it was really her when I focused on her little face and saw again the angst and hunger that covered it. Her eyes were as haunting now as they had been then.

Her nickname is Nené. We sat together on the pavement of the mausoleum of my uncle and gave her two teddy bears, a jigsaw puzzle, and a coloring book. And then, I showed her the print of my painting. She gave the painting a blank look.

"Hanapin mo nga d'yan kung nasaan ka....dito ka eh. Ituro mo nga....Naaalala mo ba 'tong picture na kinunan ko last year?"

[Look for yourself in this picture...can you recognize yourself here?

Do you remember this picture I took a year ago?] I asked with a smile.

She pointed at her face using her dirty forefinger with the dirt around her nail thick enough to plant a mongo seed. Nené's full name is Jocelyn de Guzman. She has just turned eleven a few weeks earlier. When I asked her what she did during her birthday, she simply said,

"Kumain po." [I ate on my birthday.]
"Ano ang paborito mong pagkain?"
[What is your favorite food?] I asked further.
"Jollibee po....na nasa basura.Iniipon ko po."
[Jollibee. I gather the left-overs in the garbage can,] she innocently replied.

She said that she has not tried the real Jollibee hot and fresh from the counter, all her life.

Back to the picture, I inquired if she knew the man at the center breaking bread.

"Opo si Jesus," [Yes, it is Jesus] she slowly nodded. Then I asked her what she would tell Him if she saw Him in person. This was what she tearfully said:

"Jesus, tulungan N'yo po ako...namimis ko po ang magulang ko."
[Jesus, please help me. I really miss my parents.]

8

I learned the situation of Nené's own mother from Aling Chato. She recounted, *"May sayad ang nanay n'yan-nasiraan ng bait. Me-an ang pangalan at taga-Divisoria. Nawala nalang 'yon. Iniwan silang dalawang tunay na magkapatid kasama 'yong tatlo nilang kapatid sa ama. 'Yong step mother n'ya nakikitinda-tinda lang. Pagala-gala nga 'yang bata na 'yan. Lumaki 'yong bata sa lola n'ya. Dito s'ya iniwan ng nanay n'ya sa biyenan n'ya dito sa sementeryo. 'Yong hawak n'ya sa litrato kapatid n'ya sa ama,"* she explained.

[Her mom is insane. Her name is Me-an and she's from Divisoria. She just disappeared. She left behind Nene and her other child with their stepsiblings on the father's side. Nene's stepmother sometimes requests for a little space from people to sell her stuff. Nene often wanders around aimlessly. She actually grew up with her grandmother with whom she was left here in the cemetery. The person she is holding in the picture is her stepbrother.]

I could not believe what I heard. She was living the life of a stray kitten being kicked around in the streets. I could not imagine myself being detached from my small children. I asked Aling Chato how the kid and her family manage to survive. She elaborated lengthily,

"Batang lansangan kasi 'yan. Araw-araw namamalimos 'yan doon sa Mayon. Alas onse na ng gabi kung umuwi 'yan. Pagala-gala sa buhay. Lahat sila hindi na nag-aral.(referring to her other siblings) *'Pag tinanong sila nuong mga kaklase nila sa San Jose Elementary dati kung sa'n sila nakatira, ang sagot nila sa sementeryo. Nu'ng una nahihiya sila tapos nasanay rin. Namumulot lang s'ya ng kinakain. 'Yong lola n'ya nagtitinda sa palengke. Tapos nag juejueteng. Kung anong oras dumating...kung hapon na, duon lang sila kakain... namamalimos din*

s'ya, tapos duon pa lang kakain. Namumunas ng kotse. Umaangkas sa jeep tapos namumunas ng sapatos ng pasahero. 'Pag stop light, 'pag pula, hihinto sasakay sila. B'yaheng Muñoz , Novaliches. Sa Mayon 'yon."

[She is a street child. Every day, she begs in Mayon. She goes home at 11:00 p.m. She wanders around. They have stopped schooling. When they are asked by their former classmates from San Jose Elementary where they now live, they would say that they stay in the cemetery. At first, they were ashamed of this, but they eventually got used to it. She just gets her food from left-overs. Her grandmother sells in the market, then plays jueteng. It is when she gets home that she and the others, including Nené, eat…if she arrives late in the afternoon, that's the only time they eat…she also begs for them to have something to eat. She shines cars. She climbs moving jeepneys and shines the shoes of passengers. When the signal light turns red, she and the rest transfer to other jeepneys traversing the Muñoz, Novaliches route. That's in Mayon.]

Then Nené narrated in a monotone, *"Nag-aalaga rin po ako ng bata. Nagbabasura din po ako. Maliit pa po ako nag-aapartment na' ko."* [I babysit my baby brother. I also scavenge around. I have worked with apartments since I was a child.]

"Ano 'yong apartment?" I curiously asked.
[What's an apartment?]

Aling Chato clarified, *" 'Yong nililibing ng rental in 5 years. Bata palang sila 'yan na ang trabaho."* [It means renting out the niches. Nene and the others have been using that as a source of income since they were young.]

She further said that 14,000 of the dead were buried in such niches, popularly called "apartments," for which 1,000 pesos was paid every five years.

"Sanay na po ako d'yan eh. Diyan na po ako lumaki," Nené proudly said.

[I'm used to it. This is the kind of life I've grown up to.]

"Minsan nakakausap mo ba 'yong mga patay diyan?" I naughtily inquired.

[Do you sometimes speak with the dead?]

"Naku hindi po!..." [Oh,no!]

Her eyes bulged.

"Pero may nakita ka nang mga bungo? O mga kalansay? Pa-minsan-minsan?" I insistently probed.

[But do you sometimes see skulls or skeletons? At least once in a while?]

"Mga bungô po meron."

[Skulls, yes.]

"Ano ang ginagawa mo sa bungô?"

[What do you do with the skulls?]

"Tinitingnan po."

[I look at them.]

"Tinitinda???" [You sell them?] (pretending I didn't hear it well)

"Tinitingnan po!..." [I look at them!] She corrected me. Her face lightened with a smile and she suddenly burst into giggles.

"Hehehehe 'kala ko tinitinda mo eh," [I thought you were selling them] I said with a laugh to relieve her tension.

I noticed that Nené was actually a beautiful girl if she were given a regular bath and proper grooming. And also if she would smile more often.

Still shocked at such a harsh life, I looked at Nene and casually questioned, *"Saan kayo nakatira?"* [Where do you live?]

"Dito po sa sementeryo. Minsan po sa kariton," she softly replied. [Here in the cemetery, sometimes in the pushcart.]

While talking to her, I realized that she would always look far away. Perhaps she was thinking about the contents of her kariton that she left with her playmates. The kariton was her family's only property. It was made by her father who usually just hangs around with his drinking and gambling buddies.

Nestor, the 34-year-old husband of Aling Chato, joined the conversation.

"Dito ang hanapbuhay ng tao, dito kaunti lang ang kinikita. 'Pag may pasa na trabaho kung may gagawing nitso, 'yon! Magkano lang kikitain namin d'yan--mga 300 pesos lang naman. Tapos minsan lang 'yon. Tapos sa alaga pagdarating, 'yong mga pamilya nag-aabot ng five hundred pesos a year. Ganito talaga ang buhay rito sa sementeryo. 'Pag may nagbayad ng alaga, matitipid mo 'yon hanggang sa may dumating ulit. Hirap sa buhay ang mga tao dito. Madalas nag-rurugby ang tao dito tapos wala nang makain. Karamihan ng mama rito grade 2 grade 3 lang ang inabot. Sa sobrang walang pinag-aralan nakakapang-holdap sila....Siyempre sa hirap ng buhay."

[Here, people earn little from their livelihood. You can earn when people pass on work to you and ask you to make niches. That would mean only about 300 pesos. That comes only once in a while. When the families come, they give us P500 for taking care of the niches. Life is really like this in the cemetery. When they give us money for taking care of the niches, we can save it up until the next payment. People have difficult lives here. People sniff rugby often, and have nothing more to eat. Most of the men here finished grades 2-3. Because they lack education, they end up stealing…. Of course that's because life is difficult.]

While drinking my bottled water, I tried to ponder what he said. These cemetery settlers may not have steady financial resources to support their basic needs but what permanently cripples them the most, disabling them from rising from poverty, is the loss of human dignity. Once stripped of their dignity -- forced to live in conditions quite close to those of the dead, people start to live like the dead. It is then that standards of living decline, value systems crumble and chaos rules.

"Kahit ganito kami, tinataguyod ko 'yong anak ko 'wag lang mamalimos." He said with dignity. *"Di bale na lang ako ang mamulot ng lata. Katuwiran ko, di naman nakakahiya 'yon e. 'Di ko kinahihiya 'yong trabaho ko kahit maglata ako....siyempre, katulad ngayon, walang pasa na trabaho. Namumulot ako ng yero-yero. Kaysa mang-holdap, di lalo mo lang pinaliit ang mundo mo. Pangtawid gutom lang ang habol namin dito. Etong gamit na 'to sa may ari to. (pointing to the old television set). May nakalibing dito, si Chesterton- 4 years old, apo ng may-ari. Pumayag ang lolo nila na dito kami tumira para 'di malungkot 'yong apo nila at para may kasama. Masyado kasing tahimik dito, baka mainip 'yong bangkay ng bata...buti nga may kasama s'ya."*

[Even though we are this poor, I try to support my child, just so that he won't have to beg. Never mind if I have to gather tin cans. At least, I tell myself, what I'm doing is not shameful. I am not ashamed about my work of collecting the cans...like right now, no work is being passed on to us. I collect iron sheets...that is a lot better than stealing which would only make my world fall apart. Ours is a hand-to-mouth existence. This television set belongs to the owner. There is someone buried here, Chesterton a four-year-old kid, the grandson of the owner. His grandfather agreed to let us live here so that his grandson would not feel lonely and would have companions. It's too quiet here, and the corpse of the boy might get bored…it would be good for him to have companions.]

I was looking for a buzzer to interrupt his long explanation. I was glancing at Nené and I saw her touching my gifts. I told her to play with them and share them with her brothers and sisters. Then Nestor continued. *" 'Yong tatay n'ya nagninitso rin once a week. Kung minsan nga wala pa, pagkakasyahin sa limang anak. Walang pakialam 'yong tatay n'yan. Madalas pa nga sa sugalan at nakatambay. Buti libre 'yong bahay nila walang bayad ang renta. S'yempre hindi naman makakapaningil 'yong mga patay."* [Her father also takes care of niches once a week. Sometimes, he barely has money; he tries to make ends meet for his five children. Her father does not really bother with them. He is often seen gambling and bumming around. It's a good thing they do not have to pay for rent. Naturally, the dead will not be able to collect dues.]

I realized that the best landlords are the dead. With them as landlords, tenants do not have the nagging problem of monthly rent. Besides, there is peaceful co-existence between both parties. There is always quiet and harmony.

I invited Nené and Aling Chato for snacks at Jollibee and the child really ate like she never did before. Chickenjoy, spaghetti, french-fries galore! It was for them like fine dining in a five-star hotel. It was a very special meal of her life. What struck me was that she did not consume everything no matter how much she wanted to. I was aware that she was still hungry, but she stopped eating, repacked the left-over food and sealed the styrofoam box as take-home meal for her grandmother. After that meeting, she returned to anonymity.

The Search for Judas, the Search for Self

As I drove myself back home in the embrace of night, I cried a bucket of tears. I asked myself what this search for Judas meant. I remembered Patch Adam's introspection:

"All of life is a coming home......all the restless hearts of the world... all trying to find a way home. It's hard to describe what I felt like then.... Picture yourself walking for days in snow. You don't even know you're walking in circles-- the heaviness of your legs in the drifts; your shouts disappearing into the wind. How small you can feel. How far away home can be..."

And as the poet Dante put it:

"In the middle of the journey of my life I found myself in a dark wood...for I had lost the right path."

Indeed, this experience with Nené struck very close to home base. I discovered that it was a quest towards my inner self. I sensed that this painting would allow me to enter into the mystery of home-coming in a way I have never done before.

Ripple Effect

My encounter with Nené was very trivial. I wondered if it even had an effect on her. Perhaps it was too dark for her to see, and she was in too deep a pit to reach out to anyone who wanted to clasp her trembling hands. After feasting with the left-over Jollibee with her Lola, what's next? Nené would grab the steering wheel of her kariton to scurry and scavenge around again like a rat. She would spend the rest of the day till the wee hours of the night to beg for money and food in the Mayon area. She is back to her routine. What I did was just a pittance, I know, but God had surely touched a part of her soul. It is beyond my knowledge and understanding how far-reaching my gestures would go.

The effects of kindness are not always visible but they are not wasted at all. Sometimes one never sees the fruits of his acts of compassion. But they are there, deep inside the soul of the one he touched...

I was impressed when I saw Nené share all the toys I gave her with her siblings and chums. I sensed that in spite of the hardened soul, there was tenderness in this tiny wounded heart. In the course of our conversation, I felt her unselfish character. I felt I was smaller than bacteria. I couldn't help but think of the material abundance some people experience, including myself. This mirage about the power of wealth is perhaps the reason why the poor are so generous with their money? Even with money, many of them are proportionally more generous. We may get the impression that because of their poverty the poor are *"mukhang pera."* [they are greedy with money] That's not true! The opposite is so. They readily give even the little crumbs that they have. I saw the widow's mite in Nené and in many poor people several times. They do not give out of abundance but out of the scarcity that they have. I noticed this twice in the course of the interview. Clearly, she had thought about others....

Joey: *Kung bigla kang yumaman anong gagawin mo sa pera?*

[If you suddenly become rich, what would you do with your money?]

Nené: *Papagamot ko po 'yong nanay ko...*

[I'll have my mother treated]

Joey: *Nag-aaral ka ba?*

[Do you still study?]

Nené: *Hindi na po.*

[No more.]

Joey: *Ba't di ka nag-aaral?*

[Why aren't you studying anymore?]

Nené: *Wala po kaming pera eh.*

[We have no money left.]

Joey: *Tumigil ka pala two years ago. Huminto ka grade one pa. Gusto mo bang mag-aral?*

[You stopped two years ago...when you were in grade one. Do you still want to study?]

Nené: *Gusto ko pong mag-aral. Kasi po 'pag nakakita ako ng nag-aaral, nalulungkot po ako eh. Matagal na po kasi akong huminto eh.*

[I still want to study because when I see someone studying, I am saddened. It's been a long time since I stopped.]

Joey: *Anong pangarap mo sa buhay paglaki mo?*

[What's your dream for yourself when you grow up?]

Nené: *Doktor po...para makatulong sa may sakit para gamutin ang nanay ko.*

[I want to be a doctor so that I can help the sick and treat my mother.]

Joey: *Nasa'n na s'ya ngayon?*

[Where is she now?]

Nené: *Gumagala po.* (and she cried)

[Wandering aimlessly.]

God also speaks through the poor not only through the pulpit in big Churches. At times, we have not listened to them because they are unlettered. The truths of the Bible can also be revealed through them. They truly inspire us and give us deep insights on what it means to be evangelically poor. Perhaps they themselves do not know what the term "evangelical poverty" means, but they live it spontaneously. It turned out that Nené was not Judas after all, but an angel of God in tattered clothing.

The Kariton is her Hapag

For Nené, the cemetery is her domain and the Kariton is her Hapag. The kariton is her life. It was her playpen and cradle when she was an infant. It was her hammock. As a growing child, it is her companion day by day. It is her ladder to reach for things. It is her car; it serves as her "mobile kitchen" of garbage food. This is her grotto where she prays. This is her nursery. This is her school. This is her blackboard. The pushcart is everything to her. The kariton serves as her activity center where she explores with rags and broken toys.

18

She learned Math on its wooden floor, by counting dirty pebbles and fossils of the dead. This is where she hides herself whenever she trembles in fear. This is her shield against any adult that might molest her. When she wakes up in the morning, this is her meal table and her cabinet where she dresses up. Some kids have different items for every different activity during the day, but for Nené, it is everything already. This can be her magic carpet that takes her imagination to different places and to Fantasy Island. This is the measure of who she is in society right now. This is all of life and all of eternity. One day if we leave her behind, and if she remains forgotten…this will be her bed of pain. This will be her deathbed.

Thoughts on North Cemetery

As of this writing, I am confined in a hospital. An IV is injected into my hand and medicine goes through my veins. I feel I'm wasting away. I can't help but think of my mortality. My own death. The inevitable law that all of us in our humanity are subject to – the law of death, the law that all mortal flesh like us, are subject to. This allowed me to penetrate the depth of sorrow a human heart can experience. It made me dwell in a land of darkness where I never dared imagine I could enter. This sort of coming to terms with my raw feelings, which took a long time, came as I learned to let go of my old notion that God would take it against me or punish me for being so questioning. Talking to God in the simplest way I could, with none of the usual trappings, led me to believe in faith that He is still with me despite his seeming absence. It was then that a gradual settling down within me started. I came face to face with the reality that there will sometimes be no logical and sufficient answer, no matter how I search for it. I just have to be prepared each day.

Thoughts about the graves in the North Cemetery gave me the creeps. It was really strange that I found little Judas in the cemetery. It dawned on me that Judas clearly represents the betrayal I do to myself every time I think of death as a defeat. I grappled with my own fears and confusions. Everyone knows he's going to die, but nobody seems to be completely and absolutely prepared for it. Nobody lives each day ready to die; life should be lived to the full each day.

This is why I have nothing but respect and awe for the thoughts of Mahatma Gandhi:

"Each night, when I go to sleep, I die. And the next morning, when I wake up, I am reborn."

When he spoke those famous words, he was inviting us all to

live our lives to the full – for after all, if we don't use the precious life we have, then we may as well be dead.

North Cemetery also speaks about the Empty Tomb. It symbolizes Christ's resurrection. And it sounds so reassuring. I refer to a God who inspires so much confidence and hope. Life is so complex and the many ambiguities of this life will always leave us with our unanswered questions. The need to understand, the need to have all the answers go gradually before the little piece of light allowed me to anticipate and firmly believe that there is still life. This thought was enough to tide me over, enough to remind me that there is indeed cause to sing, even when there is simply no rhyme and reason to it all. It has become "like fire burning in my heart," just like St. Paul when he said,

> *"We rejoice in the hope of the glory of God. Not only so, but we also rejoice in our sufferings, because we know that suffering produces perseverance; perseverance character; and character hope. And hope does not disappoint us, because God has poured out His love into our hearts."*
>
> Romans 5:3

The words came like a carved crystal...It was so reassuring...
I take solace in the words in the fiction book, "The Secret on Ararat:"

> *"If finding God's way in the suddenness of storms makes our faith grow broad---then trusting God's wisdom in the "dailyness" of living makes it grow deep. And strong. Whatever may be your circumstances-however long it may have lasted-wherever you may be today, I bring you this*

21

reminder: the stronger the winds, the deeper the roots, and the longer the winds...the more beautiful the tree."

Indeed, my journey to the North Cemetery has embarked me on a long spiritual journey in search of the place within. I realized that the road towards little Judas was not a path towards death. It was a path towards LIFE.

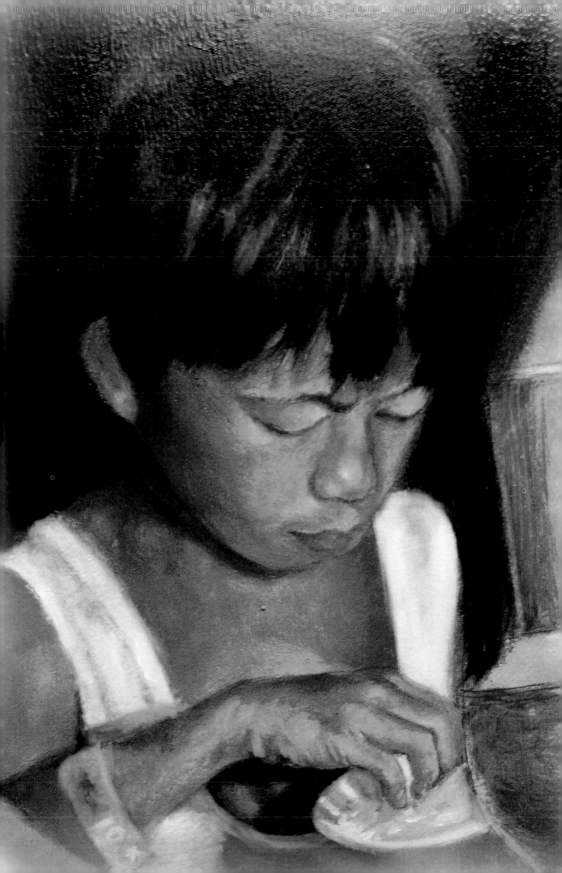

THEY HAVE JESUS

CHAPTER 2

The Bruises of Itok

"*Putang Ina mo!!!*" Linda yelled at her son Itok. [This is a Filipino curse or slanderous phrase which is close to "Son of a bitch!" but literally means "Your mother's a whore!"]

"*E di Nanay... puta ka pala?*" he brutally barked at his mother. ["So Mom…you're a whore?]

Striking a raw nerve, her mother grabbed Itok by the hair and they wrestled like animals until she pinned him down. Raging with anger, she challenged him to repeat.

"*Ano kamo???*"

["What did you say?"]

"Di ba ina kita?... E sabi mo puta ang ina ko, e di puta ka. Ikaw nagsabi noon 'di ba?" the boy snorted back.

["Aren't you my mother? You did say that my mother is a whore, then you're a whore. You were the one who said that, right?"]

This was the exchange that transpired between mother and her 11-year old son before Itok was wrung in chains in their own house. It was a show of force by a desperate mother in her desire to transform him before he becomes the next-generation criminal of Metro Manila. Rage filled their house. Broken glass. Broken dreams...

A year ago, Itok was my model for the glutton boy who was right next to Christ. He didn't even have to act or role play that part because he only had to be himself. He was literally so hungry at that time that he didn't care about what was happening around him. He didn't know all along that it was just a role and that they were posing for a modern Last Supper in the slums. I wasn't able to talk to him at all too because I was so preoccupied with the total composition and balance of the figures plus the alert capturing of the expressions on their faces. It was as if we were doing a multi-million dollar production of Les Misérables. I served them eat-all-you-can "Lucky Me" pansit Canton and bottomless juice prepared by my cook Cecille. We set the table which was made of scrap wood palette and let it stand on empty drums and other improvised materials like second hand tires. We used the old dented aluminum casseroles and pots to give a semblance of a poor people's dinner. All these were all unnoticed by Itok because he was too engrossed with satisfying his hunger. In my few glances at him, I saw him literally devouring the food. He just swallowed it like an empty gas tank being loaded with crude oil. After his amplified burps, he wiped his face in the same manner as he would wipe the windshields of cars during traffic.

Mustering quite a great deal of courage, I tore off to the cage-like house of Itok one day. They said it was a rough and dirty place. Thugs really looked mean. Their place was called 'La Dakila.' Contrary to its name, it was the hub of villains and murderous gangs that the police or politicians hire for a delicate job which they code as "operation."

"Salvage. Si Master Bong Komando Boy, sinalbage. Asset po ng pulis 'yon. Ikukulong po 'yon sa araw. Pagdating po ng gabi pinapagala. Bong Hernandez po ang tunay na pangalan. Kasama po namin sila sa Karangalan hanggang sa nakarating sila rito. Makulong po s'ya ngayon bukas laya na. Mga pulis po nag 'salvage' dun. Marami pong anak 'yon sa Karangalan. Nagtatawag po sa Batasan ng mga sasakyan..."

[Salvaged. Master Bong Commando Boy was salvaged. He was a police asset. He is usually jailed during the day. When night falls, he is made to wander aimlessly. His real name is Bong Hernandez. He has been our companion since we were in Karangalan until we got here. He gets jailed, the next day he is released. The police salvaged him. He has many children in Karangalan. He hollers for vehicles in Batasan...]

This was the account of Estokwa, a 23-year-old scavenger, the uncle of Itok. He was the one who guided me to the house of terror. Before my very eyes, I couldn't believe such a gruesome sight. With both hands shackled in a door chain, this little child Itok was growling and gawking like a young captured lion possessed by an evil spirit. He was salivating and his red eyes were sharply piercing through.

27

There was not a single tear in those brave eyes. His hands and wrists were bleeding and his fists were clenched in fury. It just made me sick to my stomach to know the cruelty he has gone through.

"All cruelty springs from weakness."
(Seneca, 4BC-AD65)

I begged her, whom Estokwa called "Hitler", to release her son. It was her only known form of discipline for a son who got involved early in robbery. According to his mother, he got hooked with three friends and was detained in the local station a couple of months ago, but he was able to escape twice using a hair pin and 'fluid.' He feared nothing on this earth. Recently, his mother was able to prevent him from another imminent detention due to alleged stealing of six sacks of palette wood from an abandoned warehouse a few nights back.

"Matigas ang ulo n'yang hayop na putang inang batang 'yan...!" [That whore's son is hard-headed...!]

The mother cried while unshakling the chains entangled to her son's widespread hands. She narrated to me how her son often got involved in perilous affairs. His group became so well known for the juvenile violence in their place.

"Wala ka namang ginawa kundi magbingo at mag tong-its buong araw...Si Tatay naman parang may pigsa palagi sa dalawang talampak-an. Upo lang nang upo palagi." Itok retorted like a hungry Rottweiler.

[You've done nothing but play bingo and 'tong-its' (a card game) all day...Our father seems like he always has boils on the soles of his feet. He just sits almost the whole time.]

"Anong pangalan mo ulit?" I verified calmly.
[What's your name again?]
"Itok. Itok Garganera po."
[Itok. Itok Garganera.]
"Ang totoong pangalan n'ya Jessie" Goliath said.
[His real name is Jessie.]
"Anong nangyari sa kanya?"
[What happened to him?]
"Kasi po 'yong isa naming kasama d'yan, si Simon, niyaya po 'yong

29

pamangkin ko tapos nagustuhan po nila...nahuli silang nagnanakaw ng paleta. Tatlong sako ng paleta. Muntik pa makulong 'yang si Itok."

[His other companion, Simon, urged him and they liked it… they were caught stealing scrap wood crates. Three sacks of palettes. Itok almost got jailed.]

I would like to believe that this very young child was hardened by the violence around him and by the events that transpired in his everyday life. A boy fails to see rightly because of a clouded mind and a huge pile of life's bruises and ugliness. While walking towards the street corner to buy squid balls, we were calming down after he had been tied up like an animal. Itok hopped so nonchalantly like a freed slave while Estokwa casually volunteered to narrate the story of his nephew...

"...maghahanap buhay po 'yang si Itok at ang kapatid n'ya. Uuwi po ng bahay 'yan. Pag dating ng alas tres may dala ng bigas at 'yong kapatid n'ya minsan, may dalawang lata ng sardinas 'pag sinuwerte. Pito po silang kakain nu'n. Maya-maya, mag-aaya nanamang lumakad para magkariton ng bandang alas kuwatro tapos makakarating kaming Montalban n'yan. Bawal kaming pumasok du'n dahil balwarte ng mga taga-Payatas 'yon e. Kami po ni Itok hanggang bago lang po kami ng tambakan dahil bawal po kami ru'n e. Gulpe po ang abot namin du'n. Sa Tungkô ganu'n din po. Karamihan ng kasama namin sa pangangal-akal may bisyo pong rugby. 'Four fingers' po na bakal ang pinangsuntok nila sa amin. Marami pong taga-Litex dumadayo rin."

[Itok and his sibling work. They return to their house. At 3:00, they bring home rice, and his sibling sometimes brings home two cans of sardines when he is lucky. Seven of them will eat that food. Afterwards, they will go out to gather things in their pushcart around

4:00, then we go on to Montalban. We can't enter that whole area because that's the bulwark of those from Payatas. Itok and I can only go as far as the dump because we are prohibited to go beyond that. We will get clobbered if we trespass. It's the same in Tungkô. Most of our companions in the trade sniff rugby. They used the steel object placed on the four fingers to hit us. Many from Litex also go there.]

"Matatapang din ba ang mga tao rito?" I cautiously asked while looking around.

[Are the people here also fierce and dangerous?]

"Marami pong gangs dito tulad ng Commando, Sputnik, M5, Akhro, Trese M, TBS (True Brown Style) mga hawak po ni Andrew E. at Francis M. Marami po akong tropa d'yan e. Basag ulo ang habol nila at away-away."

[There are many gangs here like Commando, Sputnik, M5, Akhro, Trese M, TBS (True Brown Style) under Andrew E. and Francis M. I have many groups here. They are after violent gang wars and fights.]

"Nu'ng nakaraang linggo, si Kenneth, si Onyok at Kelly pumasok po du'n sa tindahan du'n sa may kanto. Nu'ng nangalakal po kami nu'ng umaga, nakita po namin 'yong bag na itim shoulder bag ng babae 'e akala po namin, walang laman, pagbukas po namin may I.D. ng babae na nagtatrabaho po sa Land Bank. Ang apelyido po ay Borja. Tapos po, may secret saver po s'ya sa loob. May laman po na P400 tapos, andu'n 'yong mga ATM card may mga telephone numbers. 'Yong may ari po tinatawagan namin walang sagot. Dinala po namin sa may tindahan pero agad po kaming hinabol ng mga 'di kilalang tao. Wala nga po kaming mataguan eh. 'Pag umatake 'yang sina Itok, ubos 'yong tindahan,

31

ransack 'yong tindahan; nagmerienda pa sila ng mga noodles, nagkakalat sila du'n sa loob."

[Last week, Kenneth, Onyok and Kelly went inside the store near the corner. When we traded in the morning and we saw the black shoulder bag of the woman, we thought there was nothing in it. When we opened it, we saw the I.D. of the woman, whom we discovered, works in Land Bank. Her surname is Borja. Then we found out she had a secret saver card inside. It had P400; we also saw the ATM card with telephone numbers. We tried calling the owner but she did not answer. We brought the bag near the store but we were immediately chased by unknown people. We did not have a place to hide. When Itok and the others attack, there is nothing left inside the store; it's ransacked. They even eat the noodles and leave things scattered around.]

"Si Mr. Bimboy Diaz 'yong may ari po ng hardware dito sa may La Dakila, pumarada po 'yong kotse n'ya. May pera po sa loob. Bente sais mil. Muntik din po nilang manakawan 'yon eh. Nilipad lang po'yong mga pera sa kanal."

[Mr. Bimboy Diaz, the owner of the hardware store in La Dakila, parked his car. There was money inside amounting to P26,000. They almost succeeded in stealing it. The wind blew the money into the canal.]

The Dangerous Life of a Child-warrior

Itok started telling his own piece of story.
"Nangangalakal po ako.
Nagstart po ako nu'ng eight ako.

Wala pong trabaho ang mga magulang ko. Umiinom at nagsusu-gal naman ang Nanay ko. Tong-its at bingo.

Pangalawa po ako sa lima. Ako lang po ang nagtatrabaho.

Umaga pa lang po naglalakad na po ako papuntang Payatas, tapos nangangalakal na po ako. Di na po ako nakakapag- almusal eh. Sa gabi po, nagbabasura pa rin po ako hanggang alas nuebe. Alas singko po ako nagigising."

[I trade. I started when I was 8. My parents do not have work. My mother drinks and gambles. She plays tong-its (a card game) and bingo. I'm the second among five. I'm the only one who works. Early in the morning, I walk going to Payatas, then I trade. I don't get to eat breakfast anymore. At night, I collect stuff from the garbage until 9:00. I wake up at 5:00 a.m.]

"Ano ang pangarap mo sa buhay"

[What is your ambition in life?]

"Gusto ko pong maging abogado para po makatulong...parang 'di po kasi pantay pantay ang pagkagawa sa atin ni Jesus eh..."

[I want to be a lawyer so that I can help...it seems Jesus did not make us equally.]

"Many suffering people want to love God, but cannot see past their tears," says Philip Yancey. They feel hurt and betrayed. Sadly, the Church sometimes responds with more confusion than comfort.

"Pumapasok ka ba?"

[Do you go to school?]

"Grade 5 po dapat ako. Nalulungkot po ako dahil mahirap po ang buhay ngayon eh. Pinipilit po nila akong magtrabaho para po may

33

makain po kami. 'Pag 'di po ako nakapagtrabaho, pinapalo po ako ng dos por dos minsan po wire pa nga po eh. Putol po na wire. Minsan nasusugatan ako, minsan hindi."

[I should be in grade 5. I'm sad because my life now is difficult. I force myself to work so that we would have something to eat. If I don't work, I'm beaten with a hard piece of wood, sometimes with wires. Broken wires. Sometimes, I get injured, sometimes not.]

"Magkano naman ang kinikita mo?"
[How much do you earn?]
"Sa isang araw, kumikita ako ng 80 pesos. [In one day, P80]
Bumibili po ako ng kalahating kilong bigas . Minsan kamoteng may asukal na lang po ang ulam namin." [I buy a half kilo of rice. Sometimes, our viand is camote (sweet potato) with sugar.]

He spoke fast with his mouth filled with a herd of fish balls wrestling against each other mixed with an ocean of hot sauce and flour.

"Kariton po ang gamit ko. Minsan po, wala akong mahanap eh. Sa gabi po ako bumabanat 'pag wala po akong mahanap sa umaga, nag-babasura po ako. Minsan nga po nahuhuli pa po ako eh. Kinukulong po ako ng dalawang araw. Ilang beses na po ako nakulong eh."

[I use the pushcart. Sometimes, I can't find anything. At night, I exert much effort when I can't find anything in the morning; I collect stuff from the garbage. Sometimes, I am caught. I am jailed for two days. I have been jailed several times.]

It has always annoyed me to talk to people who sprinkled me with saliva as they spoke. This time, it was really worse. He was narrating his life while he picked his nose two inches deep as if extracting a slug of a .45 caliber from the cut of a soldier fatally wounded in battle. He didn't care if he damaged his blood vessels inside his double barreled nose with his claws just to pull out those calcified plaques. When he failed, he applied pressure by covering one of the barrels, and like a cannon would throw a solid mass faster than the speed of light. I thought his brains were spattered out too.

"Anong ginagawa mo sa bilangguan?"
[What do you do inside the jail?]

"Kinakausap po ako ng mga preso. Sinusuntok po ako. Inuuntog 'yong mukha ko tapos pinapakain po ako ng ipis."
[The prisoners talk to me. They box me. They bump my face against the wall, then they make me eat a cockroach.]

"Hinawakan po nila ako at pinipitpit po 'yong kamay ko. 'Wag daw po akong magnanakaw.Sinubukan nga po akong tirahin sa puwit. Buti po sumigaw po ako. Tapos dumating 'yong pulis."
[They hold me and beat my hand. They tell me not to steal. They tried targeting my buttocks. It's a good thing I was able to shout. Then the police came.]

He spoke with so much fury and anger, his eyes sharply piercing through again. In his young age, he was so fluent with the street lingo. His body movement spoke like that of a bull fighter as though he wanted to strangulate a foe.

"'Yong iba ko pong kasama, nang-iisnatch po eh. Karamihan sa amin dito sa La Dakila na magulang nag-didispatcher ng jeep.

35

'Pag nakukulong po ako, sinasaktan po ako ng pulis. Madalas po natutulog kaming gutom. Nagdarasal po ako sa gabi sabi ko sana kunin N'ya na ako...sa hirap po ng buhay."

[My other companions, they snatch. Majority of our parents here in La Dakila are dispatchers of jeeps.

When I am in prison, the policemen hurt me. Many times, we sleep on empty stomachs. I pray at night that God may take me because life is so difficult.]

He cried profusely and found it hard to breathe. I began to realize that "the warrior was a child..."

"Lahat po ng kapatid ko may diperensiya. 'Yong isang kapatid ko, kuya ko, lumalaki ang ulo,' yong si Rudolph naman nasagasaan po yon, di makalakad. 'Yong si Ryan naman po, pinanganak na walang butas sa puwit. Sa tiyan po lumalabas ang tae. Inopera po sa tiyan.' Tas 'yong kapatid kong bunso si Neneng nahulog po sa inodoro sa singit naman naapektuhan. Naipit po 'yong ugat. Nakakalakad na rin po. Paika- ika."

[All my siblings have defects. My older brother's head continues to increase in size, while my other brother Rudolph was run over; he can't walk. Ryan, on the other hand, was born without an anus. His bowel comes out of the stomach. He was operated on the stomach. And then my sister Neneng fell off the toilet bowl and was affected in the vaginal area. Her vein was pressed. She can now walk. She limps.]

At times, I ask: How can God allow pain and suffering? Why do people live hell on earth? How can there be a good and loving God, who is powerful and in control, when children suffer so much in this world? These are the perennial questions that continue to baffle us every time we meet people who suffer so tremendously. It is quite difficult to answer but I guess it has something to do with the character of oneness He has endowed us with. We have each been given free will and whatever we do, whether it is good, bad, kind or cruel, will affect the fellow next to us. This is a set-up where God will not intervene because He will encroach on the very nature by which He has lovingly made us. I have quite understood this since my high school days, but these thoughts are hard to come by when you actually see disaster right before your very eyes and you smell the sting of broken humanity right before your nostrils. Much more so when you live in such a place and eat misery by the day.

"Nagnanakaw po ako sa mga junk shop. Nagnanakaw po ako ng bakal. Minsan nahuhuli ako ng may ari ng junk shop banda du'n sa labas pa po ng Payatas. Minsan po nakakarating ako ng San Mateo. Init, ulan, nabundol na nga po ako ng jeep eh. May tahi na ako sa t'yan eh. Video karera at basketbol ang laro ng tatay ko. Ang lakas po n'yang manggulpi. May hiwa nga po ako sa ulo eh. Hinampas ako ng bakal ng belt ng tatay ko."

[I steal from junk shops. I steal steel bars. Sometimes, I am caught by the owner in the area outside Payatas. Sometimes, I reach San Mateo. Rain or shine, I was even hit by a jeep. I have a stitch on the stomach. My father plays 'video karera' and basketball. He clobbers powerfully. I have a cut in the head. He hit me with a steel belt.]

"Malakas loob n'ya manggulpi ano?"
[He hits powerfully, right?]

"Minsan nga po 'yong daliri ko puputulin ng plais. Iipitin. Lalo na

37

nu'ng binuksan naming 'yong video karera.. Kinulong po ako sa loob ng video karera nu'ng mama. Minsan nga po lulunurin ako sa drum eh. ' 'Yong nandu'n ako sa kanila du'n sa harap ng apartelle."

[One time, he was going to cut my finger with the pliers. He was going to crush it. Especially when we opened the 'video karera.' He locked me inside the "video karera.' One time, he was going to drown me. That was when I was with them in front of the apartelle.]

He picked a sharp stick from the plastic container and started piercing the bloated deep-fried fish balls himself again as if catching small fish from the river. He ate eight sticks in all. He asked me if the interview was over so that he could leave with his uncle for a second junk hunting round. It was dark when we parted. I gave him some money and he grabbed it with his sticky hand. I was left with the vendor to settle the payment.

"Kilala n'yo po sya? Bakit n'yo po s'ya kinausap?" Inquired the fish ball man who was computing silently the amount I was supposed to pay.

["Do you know him? Why did you talk to him?"]

"Wala naman. Inalam ko lang ang buhay n'ya. Naparusahan nga ng magulang kanina kaya pawis na pawis." I casually replied.

[Nothing. I just wanted to find out about his life. As a matter of fact, he was punished by his parent that is why he is sweating profusely.]

"Kilabot ng mga paslit 'yan dito. Ngayon lang ho nagalit ang nanay n'ya d'yan dahil muntik na namang makulong. Madalas ang kakampi n'ya Nanay n'ya."

38

[He is the terror of the young children. This is the only time his mother got angry with him because he almost got imprisoned again. His mother is oftentimes his ally.]

"Ha?... Mukhang alam na alam mo ha?"
[Really?...It seems you know his story very well?]

"Sikat na sikat po dito 'yang si Itok. Napakabata pa po n'yan nag tutulak na ng droga. Onse anyos lang po. Tatay po nu'n dating pulis. Natutong humawak ng pera. Sabik po makahawak talaga ng pera. Ilang beses po nahuhuli at nakukulong. Nagugulat po kami dahil kahit padlak ng kulungan kayang buksan. Padlock po ng jewelry shop nabubuksan. Ang lupit po ng batang 'yon. 'Yong jeep ni konsehal dito nabubuksan. 'Pag nakakita ng barya sa loob ng kotse asahan n'yo po ' pag napadaan du'n 'yon, mawawala 'yong barya du'n tatanggalin n'ya sa kotse' yon. Lagi pong may dalang alambre 'yong bata na 'yon, hairpin. Kwento nga po s'ya na du'n sa may bayan kumana po sila du'n ng jewelry shop. Wala po s'yang nakuhang mga ginto . Mga pera po marami. Pati 'yong mga padlock ng numero alam n'ya po' yong buksan e. Matalinong bata e. Tapos 'yong malalaking padlock, alam n'ya rin kung paano pasabugin. Nilalagyan lang nila ng fluid tapos sisindihan kusa raw pong bubuka 'yon. Kahit makulong nakakawala rin. Nangangalakal din po 'yon. Sa subdibisyon po ayaw sila papasukin ng gwardya. Gagalaw lang nang konti 'yon nandu'n na sa loob. Ang lupit nu'ng batang ' yon. Ang bilis ng kamay ng batang ' yon."

[Itok is very famous here. He is pushing drugs at a very young age of 11. His father is a former policeman. Itok learned to handle money. He is eager to hold money. He has been caught and has been jailed many times. We were surprised that he could even open the padlock in jail. He can open the padlock of the jewelry shop. He is

39

merciless! He can open the jeep of the counselor. When he sees loose change inside a vehicle, you can be sure that the money will disappear; he'll steal it. He always brings a hairpin with him. Someone related that he and his companions broke into a jewelry shop near the town. He was not able to get any piece of gold. He got a lot of money. He can easily figure out the numbers on the padlock. He is very cunning. He can also open the big padlocks and knows how to blow them up. He pours liquid on them, lights them up and the padlocks will automatically open. Even if he is jailed, he easily escapes. He also trades. The guard in the subdivision does not want to let him and his companions enter. He just makes some moves, he somehow manages to get in. He is really merciless! His hand moves fast.]

"May pag-asa pa kaya s'ya?"
[Does he still have a chance?]

He answered like a sage. *"Depende sa takbo ng buhay kung may pag-asa pa' yong bata na 'yon. Grabe 'yong bata na' yon. Nakikialam po 'yon ng mga sigarilyo, alak, pera nangunguha s'ya. Mga itlog. Kinabukasan po ibebenta rin nila 'yon sa kabilang tindahan. Minsan po nahuli sila sa loob ng tindahan nagmemerienda sila sa loob. Nahiligan po nilang gawin. Hoodlum 'yan paglaki. Sigurado."*
  "Umaakyat pa po ng tuktok ng poste 'yan kahit live nilalagari po nu'n. Sumasabog 'yong wire. Puputulin po 'yong wire tapos po tatansuin nila ' yong wire na 'yon. "
[It depends on how life turns out whether he will still have a bright future or not. He is something else! He steals cigarettes, liquor and money even eggs. The next day, he sells them in the other store. One time, he and his companions were caught inside the store eating snacks. It became a habit. He's a hoodlum. For sure.

He climbs to the top of the electric post even if there is a live wire; he will cut a live electric cable. The wire explodes. He cuts the wire then sells it as junk copper material."]

After giving me the change, the vendor walked away tired with a few pieces of the uncooked squid balls and quikiam left in his plastic bag. He was whistling with contentment for a full days' work.

It was an exhausting experience to witness the unimaginable harsh and bitter existence of a boy. It was a depressing sight. To enter a place which was like a hell's gate, was an easier task than to enter a hardened boy's heart. Any ounce of optimism will easily be waned. I was vexed with some questions that nagged my mind. Could he have been an outstanding student if he were in school? If he was at La Salle Greenhills or Xavier, could he have been good in Math? With his strength and agility, could he have been a varsity player? If he was fed with Promil when he was a baby, could he have been a gifted child? A wonder kid? This mirage is just part of wishful thinking. We all know that it is not the reality...because he was born poor...

The mother of Itok will just smirk in utter ridicule at the beautiful prose "Children Learn What They Live" by Dorothy Law Nolte. A more appropriate theme about brutality and unspeakable cruelty would be "How to Raise a Wild Pitbull" by the PBS (Pitbull Breeders Society):

"Show love by hitting him on the head with a
mallet each morning,
Show some sweetness by twisting and dislocat-
ing his bone,
Show gentleness by forcing a metal can over his

41

mouth,
Show greatness by putting him in a tight cage.
Show madness by releasing his collar...for it will
kill you."

Softening the Stance

I went home with a heavy heart and a bottle of beer. I curled
into my sofa and thought about what transpired in the kingdom of
Itok. I saw brokenness but I also witnessed the hard stance a child
like him can have. At times, I thought, I could be as stubborn and as
hardened like him. My very pride and my selfishness most often than
not stiffen and benumb me. At times it backfires at me.

When I was in grade school, I was also a tough kid. A myth was
spread in our campus that I was a grandson of a general. As a result,
many of the students feared my presence. I terrorized kids of my age
and even reached the point of asking One Peso protection money
from each kid who entered the comfort room. But one thing they
never asked was the name of my lolo. Nobody knew that my lolo and
his horse were already dead a century ago. He was none other than
--- Gregorio Del Pilar or Lolo Goyô.

I also remember the day when I ended being a bulldog. I was
busy bullying a nerdy boy when a government helicopter suddenly
landed on the football field. I was curiously watching and feeling
the spin of the big blade which looked like a big electric fan, while
my hand clenched the collar of that weakling kid. Lo and behold! A
military officer in fatigue had descended together with his camou-

flage-clad cohorts. "Dad! What a surprise!" the boy said while the father hugged his son whom he visited on his way to Clark Airbase in Pampanga.. The horses of Tirad Pass came chasing the fast beat of my heart while I shivered....

I see myself again in the character of Itok. The hard stance; the fixedness; the stubbornness and hardness. Those moments when I was trying to prove myself right and others wrong. A character of mind which was narrow and sometimes close; those events when I seemed to be impenetrable...because of pride. In our journey, we always encounter the struggle and the forces of pulling us apart from our being good and being bad. In our hard stance, there's always a corresponding softness. A great theologian once said in his poetry:

"When I fling wide the windows of faith
---now I see Him, now I don't.
Now I pray fervently, now I behave so indifferently.
Within me sleep a sinner and a saint; I know one must die if I am to live.
Everything seems to be adventure and danger in life --- on this account.

When the saint in me seeks after God,
God comes running after me.
When I run after a dream, that very dream chases me.
When the sinner in me thirsts for friendship,
selfish attachment goes hard at my heels.
When the sinner in me seeks after love,
passion grips me in its arms.
What a hair's breadth of a difference lies

between the sinner and the saint!"

A 'Salvaged' *Kid

I would like to end this part with a heart rendering eulogy of a mysterious social worker who is hidden under the name 'Barcadios.' He wrote this piece, which was never delivered nor published, for a 'salvaged' boy found in Dagat-Dagatan, Navotas, Manila in 1995. The corpse cannot be identified; the teeth were burned into ashes; the body was decayed and mangled beyond recognition. Only his tattered and nearly ashened short pants proved that he was a boy.

> *"We do not know this boy's real name and we never will. We do not know where he was born, or precisely how he lived. We do not know where in our country he had made his 'kariton' or when he pushed it when he was old enough to scavenge and collect junk in the streets. We do not know his age or his circumstances - whether his parents were from Luzon, Visayas or Mindanao. We do not know who loved him or whom he loved. If he had friends, we do not know who they were. His family is lost to us as he was lost to them.*
>
> *Yet he has always been among those we have pitied. We know that he is one of the 250 million hungry kids around the world who are forced to work for survival. One of the 24 million people in the Philippines who cannot afford food, shelter or clothing. One of the 8,000 murdered and whose cases are unsolved.*
>
> *He remains to be a harrowing statistic.*
>
> *He is all of them. And he is one of us. He can even be our own son.*

---

* **Salvage** is a slang word for summary execution in the Philippines. The meaning evolved from frequent usage in sentences similar to 'The corpse was salvaged from the Pasig river' from "salvage" meaning recovered or found. The victim would usually be a victim of summary execution. The word may also be related to the Spanish-derived Tagalog slang "sinalbahe" (literally "turned bad").

This Philippines and the Philippines he knew are like foreign countries. The tide of events since he existed has been so dramatic, so vast and all-consuming; a world has been created beyond the reach of his imagination.

He may have been one of those who believed that garbage collecting would be an adventure too grand to miss. At an early age, he may have felt that he would never live down the shame of not hunting for food as his peers did. But the chances are that he went for no other reason than to feed the empty stomach of his brothers and sisters.

Because Poverty was a mad, brutal, awful struggle caused more often than not by greed and corruption; because the waste of human life was so terrible that some said life was scarcely discernible from death; and because the adults who were supposed to lead and feed, in fact sowed the seeds of a more, even more terrible, disaster - we might think that this boy lived a wasted life.

But in noticing this ragamuffin's one per cent of goodness which he surely had, we believe that this is not true.

For out of the misery came a lesson which transcended the horror and tragedy and the inexcusable folly.

It was a lesson about poor people - and the lesson was that they were not actually poor. They are rich in things money cannot buy.

On all sides they were the heroes of the streets: not the rich in the posh villages, but the child worker - those who really endure hardship in their tender age, those who show courage, those who were bold as well as resilient, to believe that they can survive.

The unknown boy we bury today didn't have a clear idea of what was right and what was wrong. His deeds proved that real nobility and grandeur belonged not to empires and nations but to the little people in their homes as small and smelly as the pig pen.

That is surely at the heart of every poor person's story, the disparity between the rich and the small, the never ending misery...in life and in law. It is the desire to survive, the tradition in which poor Filipinos have gone through in our history.

The shredded cadaver of this child is not honored here to glorify poverty and hunger over prosperity; or to assert a boy's character above an adult's; or a street kid above a school bus-complexion-boy; or men above women; or the war of poverty in which he fought and died above any other war; or of one generation above any that has or will come later.

The Unknown urchin honors the memory of all those men and women who laid down their lives to feed the mouth of their loved ones.

His chain is a reminder of what we have lost in hunger and what we have gained.

We have lost millions of lives for the lack of food and money, and with them all their love for life in this country and all their hope and energy.

We have gained a legend: a story of a dirty rag and the sacrifice of the insignificant and with it a deeper faith in ourselves and the appreciation of every little blessing, and a deeper understanding of what it means to be Filipino.

It is not too much to hope, therefore, that this unknown boy might continue to free the others from the clutches of poverty and great misery. He might enshrine a nation's love of peace and remind us that in the sacrifice of the anonymous and unknown children of the streets...*there is faith and love enough for all of us."*

THEY HAVE JESUS

CHAPTER 3

The Mosquito of Emong

Leaping from the shadows into the dimly-lit highway of Commonwealth, the matchstick-thin silhouette of a boy waves his arms frantically at passing cars. Ten-year-old Emong is just one of Novaliches' many *'Kalakal Boys.'* He is far from home - a place called *"Kalinisan"*- 5 kilometers away. His only asset is the empty push cart he pays "rent" for, to bigger boys. He and his companions stopped renting the side cars because they have become so expensive. It's only a temporary possession until it's filled with bottles, metals, scrap cardboards which they call "assorted." He was like a guerilla "keen to the rustle of the leaves…" He also gets his chance at night after a bad catch, from passers-by... perhaps tossing him a coin...perhaps not.

"*Boy, gabi na. Ba't di ka pa umuuwi?*" [Boy, it's already late. Why have you not gone home yet?] I asked from the window of my car while glancing at my watch.

"*Wala po kasi kaming masyadong nakuhang bakal puro plastic lang po ng mineral water...*" [It's because I have not gotten a sufficient number of steel bars yet, just plastic bottles of mineral water.] he replied.

"*Naalala mo pa ba'tong picture na ito?*" [Do you still remember this picture?] I showed him the Hapag Reproduction.

He affirmatively smiled and said with jest, "*Ay oo nga pala, ikaw 'yong dating nagpakain sa amin ng pansit canton. Ang ganda po.... hehe....katabi ko po si Jesus...umiinom pa po ako ng juice a....*" [Oh, yes. You were the one who fed us pancit canton (a noodle dish). That's a nice picture...hehe...I was beside Jesus...in the picture. I was drinking juice.]

"*Wala ka bang mga kasama? Ba't nag-iisa ka?*" [Don't you have companions? Why are you alone?] I worriedly asked.

"*Nandoon po sila sa malapit sa Petron. Namamag-asa.*" [They are there, near Petron. Trying their luck.]

I reached into my pocket and gave him all the money I had in it. He took the P100 bill and gently said with a quizzical face, "*Ang laki po nito, kuya....*" [This is a big amount, kuya.] My response flowed straight from my heart. "*Ok lang, para makauwi ka na.*" [It's okay...so you can already go home.] He nodded his thanks. There was no "poor me" posture in his body language; he had a peaceful composure about himself that could only come from strong of faith. I did not feel the typical "what can I get from this person?" vibes that many people wear, or after receiving something, they think, "What more can I get?"

52

"Bigyan mo 'yong mga kapatid mo ha?" (Give some money to your siblings, okay?)

"Opo kuya." (Yes, kuya.)

"Nga pala…anong pangalan mo?" (By the way…what's your name?]

"Emong po."

"'Yan ba talaga ang ginagawa mo araw-araw?" [Is that what you really do everyday?]

"Opo, ito po. 'Kalakal Boys' po ang tawag sa amin. May mga kasama po akong mga bata rin po. Di na po kami nagrerenta ng side car dahil lugi po kami; lahat po ng kinikita namin sa kanila na lang po napupunta. Marami pong bata sa sahig na lang po kumakain. Sila po 'yong mga na"demolish" na galing Litex. 'Di ba po niluwagan po 'yan?" [Yes. 'Kalakal Boys' ('CommercialBoys') is the name of our group. I have companions who are young boys like myself. We no longer rent out sidecars because all our earnings go to rental payment.

Many kids just eat on the floor. They belonged to the group whose

54

shanties were demolished in Litex. They had road widening, isn't it?]

"Emong, puwede ba 'ko sumama sa inyo bukas? Gusto ko sanang makipagkuwentuhan sa inyo e." [Emong, may I go with you tomorrow? I'd like to share stories with you.] I asked with interest.

"Ha?...o sige po. Magsuot po kayo ng mahaba dahil mainit po at t-shirt pantakip sa mukha." [Ha?... okay. Please wear a long-sleeved shirt to protect you from the heat of the sun, and also bring a t-shirt to cover your face from the dust] he cautioned me.

"Ok 'yon. Magkita tayo. Agahan natin para makarami kayo." [That's okay. Let's see each other. Let's be early so we can accomplish more.]

We decided to meet at a gravel and sand shop in front of Diamond Motors. He waved his hand saying, *" Sige po kuya. Bukas aantayin namin kayo."* [Okay, kuya. Tomorrow, we'll wait for you.] It was an experience filled with so many surprises. Wearing a thin t-shirt and ragged, cotton shorts, he walked back to his cart excited to bring home his day's bounty. His torn slippers flopped behind him as he disappeared in the dark.

Before dawn, I was tying my sneakers and gathering all the paraphernalia I would need for that day. I met Kelly, Joshua, Tugik, and Jerly. We hopped from one junk shop to another; from one house to a public school to a small garbage shop. It was also a tiring experience but a very enjoyable and challenging one. I reminisce my childhood days with my friend Kim when we would also push the cart as assigned garbage collectors and bring all the trash to the incinerator.

It brought back those days when I would carry heavy drums and old tires to burn them in the furnace. Kim had to protect the small animals like the stray kittens, "bubulis" and hamsters, even the spiders from being shoveled down to the pit. Those were the days when we were being trained in the Juniorate of San Fernando Pampanga where our parents had to pay for our own hard labor. This time, it was for real because these boys had to do it in order to survive.

They took turns narrating their stories. *"Yong ilog po kasi na 'yan binababa namin 'yan sabay-sabay. 'To si Joshua kasama po 'yang mga 'yan. 'Yan pong maliliit na 'yan ang tinatawag po naming 'kataba.' Kinukuha po namin 'yan pang pares namin sa kanin pero alam po naming hindi nakakain 'yan. Pinapaksiw namin 'yan. Minsan naman po haha luan ng malunggay po."* [We go to that river at the same time together with Joshua and company. We get those fish which we call 'kataba'. We get them and pair them with rice even though we know it's not edible. We cook them in vinegar and sweet sauce. Sometimes, we mix them with a vegetable called malunggay.] Kelly explained how they would dive into that river connecting to Angat Dam. According to him, many kids their age were drowned while swimming and hunting creatures under water.

Jerly pointed his fingers towards a distant spot like a conquistador who just landed on an island. *"'Pag napupunta po kami d'yan sa 'tulo' 'yong bagong paliguan po d'yan, maliligo po kami tapos 'yong ginagawa po talaga niyang si Onyok nanghihingi ng tong."* [When we go there, we go to our new bathing place called 'tulo'. We take a bath, then Onyok asks for money.]

They all laughed because Onyok was being grilled on the spot.

"Malalim ba 'yan? Mag- iingat kayo..." [Is that deep? Be careful.] I warned them.

"May malalim at mababaw. 'Yong ilog na 'yan bigla na lang pong bubulusok ang tubig d'yan galing sa taas. Maraming nadedenge tulad niyan si Arnold." [There's a portion that's deep & a portion that's shallow. That river overflows suddenly from above. Many get sick with dengue, like Arnold.]

We passed by a canteen and got some left-overs and tin cans. Emong explains this time: *"Kumukuha po kami ng lata-lata rito araw-araw. 'Yong lagayan po ng kaning baboy, pinipili po namin 'yan. 'Yong mga buto iniipon po namin 'yon."* [We get cans here every day. We gather the containers of left-overs and choose them. We gather the bones.]

As we trod the winding road down the end, I saw evidence of their resourcefulness -- the kids piled up cans in front of us and the tires of the garbage trucks would crush them, making them easier to recycle. They were all malnourished, I noticed. Emong hid his dirty fingernails as I pointed out his fancy ring. He found the ring in the garbage heap, and he told me, that he once found some money and a watch.

"Gobyerno po kasi natin masyadong naging sakim. Napabayaan na po tayo." [Our government is too greedy. It has neglected us.] Fourteen-year- old Joshua asserts himself like a grown-up man as if echoing what he heard from adults. *" 'Yon nga lang pong NFA rice binebenta ng tagbebente. Dati po katorse lang. Trese. Bihira po ang ulam*

sa amin. Kanin lang. Madalas na ulam tapos mangga na hilaw tapos 'yong tsitsirya po na tagpipiso. 'Yan po madalas naming mga ulam. Kaya po 'pag bumababa kami sa mga ilog may mga puno po ng mangga roon. Mga saging. Inaakyat po namin 'yon. Binebenta po namin ng tag-pipiso po ang isa, tapos naliligo po kami sa ilog." [The NFA rice is being sold for P20. Before, it was P14 or P13. We seldom have viands, just rice. Our usual viand is raw mango, then junkfood that cost P1 each. When we go down to the river, we climb the mango and banana trees. We sell them for P1 each, and then we take a bath in the river.]

"Inaasikaso ba kayo ng mga magulang n'yo?" [Do your parents still take care of you?] I asked with concern.

"Umaga pa lang po nasa tong-its bingo na 'yong Nanay ko." [My mom and her friends are already playing 'tong-its bingo' in the morning.]

Kelly answered in all honesty. *"Hanggang mag-aala sais ng gabi nandoon na po sila. Mga anak nila di po nila alam kung saan napunta. Meron pong mga bata kung saan-saan na nakarating. 'Yong mga barkada po nila nababarangay na."* [They play until 6:00 p.m. They don't know where their children go. There are children who reach various places. Their peers are eventually disciplined by the barangay].

Onyok was like a voice in the wilderness. *"Mga bata po na nakakasama ko sa pagbobote bakal malalakas po ang loob... matatapang, wala na nga pong takot sa kamatayan kasi po kahit sa hi-way na nagba-bike kami, kahit 'yong mineral water na plastik na nasa gitna ng kalsada, kahit may sasakyan po kinukuha nila iyon kahit mabibilis ang sasakyan. Lalu na sa hi-way na ganyan."* [The children who together with me look for bottles and steel are courageous. They no longer have fear of dying. They are ready to risk their lives just to get empty bottles of mineral water in the middle of the road, even when there's a car zooming by.]

They were saying that one big sack of plastic bottles would only cost P15 or P20 for one kilo whichever is lower. The junkshop owner will then trade them at a higher rate for recycling.

"Nakikita ko po d'yan sa mga junk shop may pumipik-up po ng mga trak tapos 'yong mga karton, mga lata, magkano lang kilo ng lata tatlong piso dalawang piso 'yong karton dalawang piso. Ang mahal lang po d'yan 'yong bakal kasi 'yong bakal po nuwebe otso po 'yong kilo noon e. Sa ngayon po, bihira ka na po makakuha ng bakal na mabibigat. Ang nakuha namin marami dyan mga pako o turnilyo naiipon po namin 'yon. Tapos lata po kahit anong klaseng lata...." [In the junk shops, I see someone pick up the cartons, the cans and place them in the truck. One kilo of cans costs only P23; a kilo of cartons P2. It's only the kilo of steel bars that commands a high price...P8 – 9 per kilo. Right now, it's difficult to get heavy steel bars. Many of the stuff we've gathered are nails or screws; we've gotten cans, different kinds of cans.]

After the work as Kalakal boys, they sell pandesal around the villages and earn a meager amount of P10 each. *"Sa umaga po mga alas dos nakaabang na sila sa bakery tapos pila-pila sila roon nagpapalista ng pangalan tapos kanya-kanya po sila ng mga box. Pagdating ng alas siyete mauubos 'yong pandesal nila tapos ayun makikita n'yo po sila sa may tindahan kumakain ng kanin, tapos ang ulam po nila tsitsirya tagpipiso po tapos boy bawang ganoon."* [Around 2:00 am, they wait in the bakery, each with his own box, line up and register their names. At 7:00 am, their pandesal runs out, then you'll see them near the store eating rice and snacks costing one peso each and roasted cornick as their viands.]

"Tapos basketbol sila tapos kara cruz. Tapos mawawalan na naman po ng mga pera 'yan. Tapos balik na naman sila ipon-ipon. Nandoon na naman sila sa bakal. Sa bike na naman sila o sa ganitong kariton ganoon na naman ang ikot ng buhay namin." [Then they play basketball, afterwards, 'kara cruz'. Then they run out of money again. Then they gather more stuff. They go to places where they can get steel bars. They bike or go around in pushcarts like this. This is the cycle of our lives.]

We stopped at a nearby bakery at dusk to eat some mamon and hopia. *"Pers time naming makakain ng masarap na cake. Sa basura po kasi kami kumakain 'pag dating ng hapon. 'Yong mga bulok-bulok na balat ng repolyo at sayote ginugulay namin 'yan."* [It was our first time to eat delicious cake. When afternoon comes, we eat from the garbage. We eat the rotten cabbage and sayote.]

While sipping some cold coke and Sprite, we shared our different views about the painting where Emong drinks juice beside Jesus. I was startled with Emong's naïve and pure interpretation of it.

"Uy! 'Yong mga bata inimbitahan si Hesus na kumain. Nakita po nila napagod 'yong Diyos kaya pinagpahinga nila." [Hey! The kids invited Jesus over to eat. They saw Him dead tired and so they let Him rest.]

" Hehe. Oo nga ano?" [Hehe. That's right.] We all laughed and he received a *"Kutos"* [a knock on the head] from each one.

I paused with such a cunningly powerful message. The comment stayed with me for quite some time because it was seen from a different angle. We parted ways before dusk in the hope that a new friendship sprung forth. It had been a tiring day but again I learned valuable lessons from their simplicity of their life.

They Invited Jesus

While chewing the cud of what he said, I realized it may also be true. In this Last Supper, it is not a banquet of Jesus. This is a banquet of poor kids who invited Jesus to dine with them. He is the Guest of honor. He is a special Guest. Because He is the main Visitor, He was given the best place at table. The Filipino from all walks of life is always hospitable. The values take precedence. Even thieves and criminals hold that innate value. Be my guest. Rest for a while. *"Kumain ka na ba?"* [Have you eaten yet?] or *"Kain tayo."* [Come let's eat.] While you might think that normally we are focused on Jesus who gives these poor pathetic kids a special meal, it is not so. It is the other way round. In their meager resources, they prepared a meal and they found Jesus alone and tired that's why they invited Him. Christ is not sad here. He is just too tired. These kids give him a good massage on His shoulders with their tiny fingers and serve Him with soup that almost spilled on His cloak. They give the primal place to Him.

Sometimes we approach Jesus. We go to His place. We don't usually invite Him. We are expecting Him to invite us. We don't usually say, "May we invite you." Or "Dinner is served, Jesus." *"Handa na ang hapag."* [Dinner is ready.] Sometimes we think so. There are times that many of us spend our lifetime looking for and going to Je-

sus. There are also times when Jesus simply says 'I want to be invited."
"Ako naman ang gustong pumunta," if only you will open your heart.

He was dead weary in that painting, that was why he was
brought by the kids to sit and eat. He was served the best food and
they wanted Him to rest. Who among us approaches Christ with the
desire to let Him rest a while? Usually we call on God because we
want something. We are the ones who want rest. We are tired. There
are pure and innocent people who might think this way. They want to
give something to Him. Who among us will go to a church and kneel
down and change the God-I-need-something formula for prayer?
Can we also say, God do you need something? Even if He doesn't
need anything because He is God. Is there anything I can do? I kneel
down. Lord I'm here. *"May magagawa naman ba ako para sayo?"*
[Is there anything I can do for you?] When did you call a friend and
say out of the blue, "How are you buddy? Can I do anything for you?
[Even when he does not ask for it; even when he does not need it]
"P're kamusta, may magagawa ba ako para sa iyo?" [Buddy, is there
anything I can do for you?] You need anything? When was the last
time we did that? When was the last time we did that to God? In the
meal, we are the ones served by God. When did we organize a meal
that our only motivation was to celebrate it with God and serve God
saying, "Lord, what can we do for You?"

We parted ways before dusk in the hope that a new friendship
sprung forth. It had been a tiring day but again I learned valuable lessons from their simplicity of life.

The Slippery Time

My orientation is entrepreneurial in nature. I grew up in the business arena and I had been running my small company since I was 21 years old. In business, punctuality is the name of the game.

I have become so time-conscious. Things have to be done on time. Deadlines have to be met at all costs. "Luncheon meeting starts at 12," so I have to be in the lobby at 11:30. "Delivery is on Friday." So I have to get all the stocks ready on Thursday morning. In production, we label job orders as "Rush" and sometimes "Mega Rush" cum exclamation point. Time was at the tip of my fingers. I always did magic. My life then revolved around the clock.

When I met the Kalakal boys, they did not actually arrive on time. I felt jittery at first but I discovered something. They do not run by the measurable tick of the clock. They run by their READINESS. The kariton leaves when all the 'tropa' are ready. So it could wait for one hour for an eight-hour trip. They do not have a fixed time because some sleep late due to shifting, *"Napuyat po ako dahil walang mahigaan. Inantay ko pa po magising 'yong kuya ko para ako naman ang makahiga."* [I stayed late last night because there was no space to sleep. We are crowded in our small room. We do 'shifting' when sleeping.] One of them had to leave with an empty stomach. *"Di ako nakaalis agad. Wala pong natirang pagkain kagabi. Simot lahat."* [I wasn't able to leave right away. There was no food left for me. Everything was consumed.] Another boy, the latest to arrive, excused himself by saying, *"Inubos ko pa po 'yong tinda kong pandesal kaninang madaling araw para may pandagdag na pagkain para kay bunso."* [I sold all the pandesal I had early this morning so that I would have additional

63

food for our youngest.]

My observation was that they moved as long as they were pre-pared and ready. The trip does not start at a specific hour but when they are all gathered around. At that point, I decided to keep my watch in my pocket.

The Good Book has a beautiful song:

"There is an appointed time for everything. And there is a time for every event under heaven. A time to give birth, and a time to die; A time to plant, and a time to uproot what is planted. A time to kill, and a time to heal; A time to tear down, and a time to build up.
A time to weep, and a time to laugh; A time to mourn, and a time to dance. A time to throw stones, and a time to gather stones; A time to embrace, and a time to shun embracing. A time to search, and a time to give up as lost; A time to keep, and a time to throw away. A time to tear apart, and a time to sew together; A time to be silent, and a time to speak. A time to love, and a time to hate: A time for war, and a time for peace.
"What profit is there to the worker from that in which he toils? I have seen the task which God has given the sons of men with which to occupy themselves. He has made everything appropriate in its time. He has also set eternity in their heart, so that man will not find out the work which God has done from the beginning even to the end. I know that there is nothing better for them than to rejoice and to do good in one's lifetime; moreover, that

every man who eats and drinks sees good in all his labor,
it is the gift of God. I know that everything God does will
remain forever; there is nothing to add to it and there is
nothing to take from it, for God has so worked that men
should fear Him. That which is, has been already, and that
which will be has already been, for God seeks what has
passed by."
(Ecclesiastes 3:1)

Some years ago, a Scripture expert was explaining to me the
difference between our concept of time which is the Greek 'chronos,'
from the Biblical idea of time which in Greek is 'kairos'. He was
saying that in the eyes of the Bible, time is not chronos but kairos.
It is not the mechanical, measurable time but the time of readiness,
the opportune time. We are called to be vigilant in order to be ready
when the Lord comes. To be vigilant does not mean to keep looking
at our watch but to watch for the appropriate time because time is so
slippery. I was impressed and enriched with such scholarly comparison, but everything sounded strange including the concept itself. In
other words, it did not really sink in.

Emong was the less talkative in the group. They call him
"Emong Bangaw" not only because of a prominent mole on his
chin, but because of his dexterity at catching mosquitoes. I observed
Emong do it single-handedly. Most adults during my time killed
them and crashed them violently as though the insects were their size
and match. The trigger-happy spray at them. Our neighbors in our
old place in Cubao creatively devised a trap. Some used nets. Other
kids snapped them with bare hands. Emong knew the ultimate technique. Silence. Speed. Concentration.Confidence. Nobody talked.

His eyes squinted as it stared at the microscopic eye of the small creature. His right palm approached millimeter by millimeter. He didn't
breathe. And with one graceful whooping speedy motion...gotcha!

Alive, the mosquito lingered and flew around the very small
space provided by his enclosed tiny fingers and palm.

At hindsight, I can say that it was so unsanitary, but he just
taught me a lesson on how to catch time, the opportune time, the
"God experience" so to say. It is a time which becomes a moment
when it is caught. It must be done with the art of mosquito hunting...
quietly...speedily...promptly.

In the business world, we move in the fast lane. We are time-
conscious because we are money-conscious. No wonder we equate
time with money. "Time is gold" is a familiar maxim. So we let ourselves be ruled by time and money. This was how I dealt with clients
and associates. I was so time-conscious that I looked more on the face
of the clock than on the faces of clients and associates. I was cunningly staring at them with the what-do-I-get-from-you look. I was time
conscious but not people conscious. I focused on the efficiency and
the computation of time and motion than on the value of harnessing
true and lasting "relationships."

At this point, I cannot resist the temptation to share a personal
experience that happened in our family on an ordinary Sunday afternoon. It has something to do with the Biblical concept of time. It was
a very simple event which turned out to be a wonderful one. It was in
this experience that God allowed me to understand 'Kairos.'

A year ago or so, I was a real golf addict. It occupied most of
my time. I was more than a fairly regular golfer...because I played

frequently even when there was a typhoon. One stormy golfing after-noon, my two buddies and I were almost hit by lightning. The rain was coming down in sheets. I was a hot iron being immersed in cold water. In spite of my sight being blurred with the heavy down pour of water, I pulled my 7- wood from my bag and fired the ball up in the air...at all costs. The entire fairway became a huge water hazard because of the strong rains. Like blinded but undaunted warriors, we threw our wrecked umbrellas and trekked the remaining holes. The green was drowned in muddy water; there was no dry line to the cup. I firmly putted nevertheless. Scoring a par on that last hole, my only objective was to reach the clubhouse alive.

We saw this to be so challenging that we marveled about it. We bragged about this story to others like hell. We boasted about this rain-plagued game like the Spartans who gathered the spoils in the war of Thermopylae.

It was a fulfilling game, but I was so far away from home; away from my family.

One ordinary Sunday afternoon, a year later, I was in the lanai painting the first layer of the Hapag. I had not been playing golf for a long time due to my kidney illness. Then, I saw my 10-year-old son play basketball at our backyard. It was drizzling. He outgrew the rain-rain-go-a-way rhyme and the clouds began to get heavy and the rain started to pour. And so I asked him to stop! But it seemed he turned a deaf ear so I was forced to go out and pull him out of the mess. At my back, I didn't know that my two daughters were following. Before we knew it, all of us got wet splashing the puddles. From the win-dow, my wife Queeny was carrying our baby. Her frowning face was transformed into a smile and she could not resist joining us. The wind was strong.

My sight was blurred all these years from the real yet simple joys the family could bring. It was really a NICE FEELING to take time playing and catching the water in the mouth and embracing my wife and each of my four children under the rain while whispering "Thank you dear God". It was cold but inexplainable joy was on their faces. I saw a vision I would not have exchanged for anything else in the world at that time. It took us less than 20 minutes to do that but the time we spent became a MOMENT. It was a magic moment. Before that day, I had thought that true happiness could be found in the hilly and undulating fairways and in the business arena where my time was spent the most in the years that passed.

Unbelievable…It was just in our own backyard…on an ordinary Sunday afternoon.

God Experience

This was "kairos" for me. A "God experience". If I did not come out in the rain and just remained painting, I would not have embraced "kairos". If I was not vigilant enough to catch the smiles of these people I love, I would not have felt "heaven in the wild flower or seen the world in a grain of sand and infinity at a distance…." I thank God for leading me to this rare moment and privilege in my life. We only get one opportunity to use each minute we have; once it has passed, it is gone forever. We have to be swift in catching the mosquito. It flies quickly and it may never come back.

This is a great gift of the Kalakal Boys to me. They made me see time at its best. They made me pay more attention to people.

Mosquitoes have always bothered us. They buzz in our ears and they linger around us. So do poor people. But they can teach us great lessons. Sometimes, we sarcastically slight them on how they view time. The Kalakal boys' time is not having no time at all. It is paying close attention to the opportune moment, to the "kairos" rather than the "chronos".

That night, it was clear as day that God sent Emong to me to awaken me to my true self, that which recognizes unconditional love, peace and joy. Poor people seems to be constants in our society. Maybe because they provide the best opportunity for us to rediscover our abundance of blessings...and our inner goodness. Maybe when we all do, there would be no need for anyone to be poor. This encounter with him is definitely a "kairos" a home run...with all bases filled.

THEY HAVE JESUS

THEY HAVE JESUS

CHAPTER 4

Hapag of Jun and Roselle

I saw the world in the eyes of Jun and Roselle when I visited them in their mother's makeshift sari-sari store on the gutter of Franc Street (North Fairview Quezon City). These children were my models who were sitting on the rust-coated drum with hands leaning on the dilapidated wood crate made into a table. I was surprised to see both Jun and Roselle clad in the same clothes they were wearing when I took their photo a year ago. The boy's shirt became as thin as the silk screen, while the girl donned her favorite turquoise Hello Kitty dress which hanged off her frail body like a tent.

We gathered under the mango tree and they narrated to me

how they work to earn their baon for their schooling in a nearby public school.

"Tinutupi po namin 'yong drum. "'Yong puwit po niyan naba-baklas tapos po pinipitpit namin 'yan. Ibabanda namin 'yan sa gutter tapos papaluin namin ng bato 'yan tapos uupuan namin 'yan hanggang mapitpit at bumaba lalo tapos tatalunan namin," [We disassemble the drum. Its bottom can be detached, and then we flatten it. We bring it to the gutter, then hit it with a stone. We sit on it until it is flattened. Then we jump on it,] explained Junjun while gasping for breath which alternated with every word he uttered.

Roselle's turn of explaining was more elaborate: " *'Yong gulong po tinitingnan po namin kung may tama o wala, tapos p'wede pang pangreserba, binebenta po namin sa mga bulcanaysing shop. Bente pesos, kinse 'pag may tama na. Di na po p'wede kung may tama lalo na kung tubeless."* [We look at the wheel and see if it has dents. If it has none, it can be used as a reserve. We sell it to the vulcanizing shop for P20. If it has a dent, we only get P15. If it has many dents, it will not do, especially if it is tubeless.]

Jun had this story. *"Marami pong tirador ng gulong lalo na mga jak, starter at mga paleta po, may nagbebenta tatlo isang daan. Binebenta gagawing papag at kariton tapos gagawing lamesa at upuan. Madalas pong nagbebenta ng ganito 'yon pong sa may pabrika nagbebenta diyan 'yong bodegero. Talamak po diyan 'yong nakawan,"* [There are many stealing tires, and especially jacks, and even palettes are stolen and are being sold at 3 pieces per P100. They are being made into beds or pushcarts, tables and chairs. Usually, the ones who sell these are the warehousemen. Stealing is widespread.]

"E iyong mga scrap paper at karton saan n'yo dinadala?" [Where are the scrap papers and cartons brought?] I inquired in my attempt to estimate how much money they earn. Roselle quickly raised her hand shoulder high as though she was in a recitation class...

" 'Yong papel na 'yan inaayos po namin, pinopor kilo po namin 'yan 1.50--'yan po ang tinatawag naming "assorted". Dati po kinse bawat dangkal. Ngayon po kinikilo na nila. Sa gabi 'yang mga Kalakal boys. Dinarasal ko po sa Diyos humihingi po ako ng biyaya sa Diyos, sana magbago po ang buhay namin at gumanda 'yong nararanas namin." (We arrange those pieces of paper into 1.5 kilos each. We call them "assorted". Before we would sell them at P15 per unit. Now, it's being sold per kilo. At night, The Kalakal boys sell them. I pray and ask God to change our lives for the better.)

Hapag in the heart of the Family

The family of Jun and Roselle gave me another deeper insight on the role of *hapag* (referring to the meal table in the house of the Filipino) in a family. I noticed that in spite of the simple food they could afford, it was their custom to gather their family around their small dilapidated table. The hapag is the only furniture any poor family can boast of. It is central, and many things happen in that piece. It's a poor man's everything.

According to Rose, they strive as much as possible to eat together. Sometimes, when her husband is out on his tricycle route, they still feel they are complete because Roselle would pray: "Keep him safe always, Jesus." The role of a table is very important because many things take place on that four-legged structure. I failed to realize the unifying power it could give the home. Many things transpired and many things are remembered on that flat board which we call *"dulang"* and *"hapag"* in our native tongue or *"La mesa"* in our inherited Spanish language.

The deepest and the richest term is *hapag*. In a Filipino family, so many things happen at table...at the *hapag*. The table for the Filipino is a central piece where you do business; where you count money. It is there where you deal and negotiate especially the home business. In the past, there is no factory yet, so you sit and discuss production at table. The table is essential to a Pinoy's house. It is the measure of wealth; it is the measure of encounter. It is the measure of memories. There is a wealth of memories at table. It resonates to every man. That's the reason why so many people eye it for their inheritance. The Tagalog poetry says it all.

"Tanang ari-arian, sa inyo na lahat na kunin
ngunit akin ang hapagkainan."

What are our best memories? At table, isn't it? The stories of our families handed down from generation to generation are narrated during meals. Think of those moments when you come home tired. Mother waits for you and sets a late dinner for you. It is at table where mom coaches you. It is there where you do your assignment. "Junior, what's the assignment? Let's do it here." I remember it was on our empty table where I lay down one New Year's Eve pretending I was the lechon with a red apple wedged into my mouth. It broke my Mamang's heart to see her chubby child resorting to imagination and made her tear off to the market and spend her last centavo to buy a real one. Classic family anecdotes. Beautiful memories. We associate our gatherings with moments of sharing. The kare-kare, bulalo, morcon, embutido, letchon kawali galore! I feel Mamang's tender love whenever I see the old table.

The memories of your father are during table affairs. I remember my father bringing me to different places, but the best moments of children with parents are usually during meals when we eat. Recall your father whom you saw at table alone...and you sit with him. You talked about life. I vividly remember the last days of my weakening Papang on a spot where he would usually sat at our round table, just because he had a different diet. I felt disturbed with what I painted one morning as I sat on that same spot too.

It is there where you build love and concern. It was there where you were asked by your parents to feed your younger siblings. We find that in other cultures again, the table is where we are given the responsibilities towards brothers and sisters; towards fellowmen. This especially happens in larger families and in small ones, too. also. "Is the person beside you eating well, Sonny?" Interrelationship. Interdependence. The table is indeed very rich.

Where do we get scolded or *sermonized*? When we play with rice. When we put coins on top of our table. We had petty quarrels on that round battle ground too. We prayed there too. It is there where you break the news, "Dad, Mom...we're planning to get married." It is there where you break their hearts. "I'm sorry. I'm pregnant." Good news and bad news. It is there where you get healed. "Have a seat honey. Let's eat." It is also there where we see and smell hope. *"Gagaling na raw si Tatay."* [Our father will get better.]

The meal is not only social nourishment. It is family nourishment in the presence of each and everyone. That is why Jesus said, "Do this in memory of me." We remember Jesus with us during the meal. It is not only in Filipino culture, but it is in cultures all over the world as well. He ate with sinners too. He invited them at table. Jesus was so good in choosing a venue for him to be remembered--- during meals as we eat food. One will understand why in our meal, even so in the Eucharist, it is not just a question of being fed by Jesus. At table, and in the celebration of the Mass, we also feed each other. Theologically, the richness of the mass is the fact that Jesus feeds us. Not only is it so. In the Mass, we are there to pray for one another. We make each other strong. We are as if in a real table. We reach for food and we serve food to one another through our togetherness. We may not be the very food like Christ himself in the host, but we share ourselves too. That is the context of the Filipino culture too, which may give us the explanation why we always insist on our completeness whenever we eat. Just being together is more than enough.

Divine Providence

I noticed that Jun and Roselle were poor but they were happy. Upon entering their place, I was shocked because the walls were made of collaged cigarette boxes overlapping one another. Patches were all over. It was sky bright. An hour's continuous drizzle would shatter the improvised wall anytime.

And so I asked Rose, the mother of the children, if they weren't afraid the walls would crumble down. It was too dangerous and risky.

The skinny woman who had lost most of her teeth, smilingly replied, *"May awa si Lord, hindi naman po kami pababayaan."* [God has mercy. He won't let us down.] Compassion of God. *Awa ng Diyos.*

This unpredictably dangerous situation is accompanied by a firm trust in God as the Provident Father. Rose brings this out more clearly. They practically have nothing. They literally live on hand-to-mouth existence. What she said is literally true: "We live on the mercy of God." *"Nabubuhay kami sa awa ng Diyos."*

In Scripture, over 800 names and titles refer to Jesus. Yet, one name that doesn't appear in Scripture is "Compassionate God." But don't those two words say it all?" "Compassionate God" defines all the other names. Bread of Life, Carpenter, Nazarene , Lamb of God, Prince of Peace, Lord of Lords, Light of the World, Shepherd. Every second of his earthly existence, based on a desire to save the lost, was bound in compassion: compassion for his followers, compassion for those in pain, compassion for those who were blind to His truth.

These poor people hold on to this truth. That God will never ever abandon them even if the walls of this earth crumble down.

"Nasa Diyos ang awa, nasa tao ang gawa" ("Compassion is from God, hard work is from man.") is a very rich and popular Tagalog proverb very applicable to the fatalistic indolent Filipinos who idolize the proverbial "Juan Tamad" (lazy Johnny) who did not bother to go up and pick the guava from the tree. He preferred to just lie down and patiently wait till the guava would fall right smack on his face … and straight to his gaping mouth. What is up there, would eventually find its way down here. That law of gravity is what counts for lethargic people of our culture. But Rose was different. She is definitely a hard worker who just cannot get out of the rut. She perspires blood together with the farmer who breaks his back under the heat of the sun, the welder who risks his life on top of the trusses in spite of the storm, the old man in the middle of the highway uprooting an iron bar in spite of the heavy smog and pollution, the boy selling Storck

or Halls candies along the main thoroughfares of Manila earning daily P2 for 3 pieces sold. The bottom line is that Filipinos will grab whatever opportunity is out there to make a buck or two. Hard work is not the main and only issue. Provide the poor Filipinos the right incentive, the right environment and they will surely work harder than most. Rose is richer in faith because coupled with her labor, she leaves everything in the hands of the mighty Provider. She is hard-working and she sweats her brows from sun up to sun down, but poverty just lingers on.

As I continued chatting with them, they would always begin and end their sentence with "kung may awa ang Poon…" [If God will have mercy on us…]of which they are equipped with the firm faith and trust that God will not abandon them at all times. They inherited this phrase from their old people from their past generations. These are not words merely spoken, but this is their real life.

We worry about so many things in this world. Who will…?, What will…?

We are sickly insecure and fearful about tomorrow. This is normal but aren't these the problems of everyone else? Do not the Gentiles worry so? We who are Christians and living witnesses to his Word, do we not trust that God will provide, that God will take care of his own people? Do we not believe that He will not let us down later on when we are sick and when we get old? Jesus tells us in the Gospel:

"Take therefore no thought for the morrow: for the morrow shall take thought for the things of itself." (Mt 6:34)

81

Do not worry about the things that will kill your body. When Jesus sent his disciples two by two, he explicitly instructed them not to carry any extra clothing, nor a traveling bag at their back because *"a worker will not want for his wage. "*(Mt 10:10)

"Seek first the kingdom of God and all your needs will be well-provided for. " (cf. Mk 8:14 -21).

When the disciples were bickering among themselves in the boat because they forgot to bring bread along with them, Jesus rebuked them. Their worry stemmed from lack of comprehension of the breaking of the bread.

We receive the bread of life when we claim Jesus as our Savior and Lord. The sacrament, through which we receive His body and blood, tells us that God provides for His people. Jesus allowed himself to be broken that we may live fully. If Jesus can give Himself so, will He begrudge us our material needs? If we just understand the Eucharist a little bit more, we won't be so worried about our future. God will provide. He cares. Can we Christians say with Rose: *"Nabubuhay ako sa awa ni Lord?"* [I live through the mercy of God?]

As an enthusiastic entrepreneur, I have espoused the ideas of business gurus like Anthony Robbins, Bryan Tracy, Tim Warren, or our local Francisco Colayco. I was amazed with their business sense and wisdom. If you summarize all their teachings, they would boil down to one idea: goal-setting. And it indeed makes sense. There was one instance when I followed their success formula by putting everything in writing and I laid out in colored print the material things I aimed to achieve and to acquire. It was for the purpose of visualization and internalization. These things started playing in my mind through hypnosis.... "I can achieve!!!" "I can conquer!!!" Coupled with these slogans, I would play the soundtrack "Eye of the Tiger" by Rocky Balboa while I would jog in the morning.

One morning in the clinic, the diagnosis from the doctor said, "I'm afraid our news is not very good."

All goals and hopes crumbled. The earth suddenly stopped moving. There was a huge halt. The brand new four-wheel drive Range Rover in my print of dreams suddenly became irrelevant. A purchase of a prime property suddenly dissolved down the drain. Kayaking around Boracay became corny. The Rolex watch crackled and ticky-tick-tacked like a Mickey Mouse watch. The caviar or "hors d'oeuvre" started tasting bitter and could not get through my throat. The music of Rocky trembled down into monotone. All my plans for the future melted like night mists under the glare of the July sun.

It happened to a good friend of mine. One day he could choose his tee time at the most elegant golf course in the country; the next he couldn't even be the caddie. One day he could Lear jet across the country to see the different islands. The next, he couldn't afford a taxi across town. The market crashed; his assets tumbled. What was liquid went dry. What was up went down. Stocks and the strong man went broke. There he sat on his leather chair and soon-to-be-pulled-out mahogany desk when his cell phone rang with the news of a next problem in line...

Upon writing this book, I encountered several fears and "what-ifs". It is queer but I had these thoughts: What if there's a fire and I am away? What will happen to these files? They will be gone and I won't remember them. I've gone this far. So, I better save them on a disc. But what if I misplace the disc after the fire? Sending the files to my own e-mail address might be the safest. But what if I forget the password due to amnesia or what if I collapse? All my labors will be dampened to naught. I could go on and on and on. I was getting paranoid and anxious.

A gentle whisper came, soothing my mind and heart: "Everything… yes…everything is in the hands of God."

Aling Rose is right… We can only do things "kung may awa si Lord." We do not hold the future in our hands. The future depends on God. The rebuke of James in his letter comes to me *"You say, 'Today or tomorrow we are off to this or that town, we are going to spend a year there, trading and make some money. You never know what will happen tomorrow. You are no more than a mist that appears for a little while and then disappears. Instead of this, you should say, if it is the Lord's will, we shall be alive to do this or that."*(Jn 4:13-15)

Aling Rose does not know this Bible passage. She only knew about her garapon and cheap retail sales of tsitsirya but she lived this beautiful truth. Yes, it is so important to be goal-oriented and to work by objectives, but with that openness to … "kung may awa si Lord."

Jun and Roselle are poor children but they are rich in faith. They have what we call "abundance in scarcity". Their home is built with love and understanding. Simple is their life but they adore each other. They have an "alkansiya" made of bamboo and they save for the rainy days. But their most important insight which does not need much explanation, is that they enjoy each other. Nothing, not money, power, or fame, can replace family and friends or bring them back once they are gone. Our greatest joy is really our family.

THEY HAVE JESUS

CHAPTER 5

Jesus in the Slums

A priest once observed, *"You know, your painting is incorrect. None among the little apostles looked at Jesus except for that small child who barely side-glanced. The rest were focused on their own activities. In history, the Last Supper paintings including that of Caravaggio and Da Vinci, were always Christ-centered. All the characters were looking at the focal point which was Jesus. The title 'Hapag ng Pag-asa' seemed inappropriate because they were not looking at hope. They seemed hopeless. "*

He had a valid point and I was intimidated with such a statement at first, because the priest was also a good artist and he lived in Italy, the country of art and culture, for so many years.

Yes, the children were more preoccupied with filling their stomachs and satisfying their hunger in this painting. Their eyes were fixed on their plates and the food as tall as Mt. Everest, but they held on to the promise of Christ's friendship. They might have had no eye contact with each other, but each one KNEW that Jesus was with Him. They were all aware that a friend's warmth would sustain them. They were so at home with God. That kind of perspective gave them clear hope.

No one was looking at Christ. No one was looking at the light. In modern parlance, they all 'snubbed' the host of the dinner. But as I gazed more and more at Christ's presence among them, it dawned on me that Jesus did not mind at all actually. He is a God who not only pays attention to people who look at Him all the time, but also to those who don't pay attention to Him. He cares not only for those whose voices are blaring but also those whose voices are drowned in the wilderness. In his greatness, His love sheds its light to everyone unconditionally. Even if we run away, He will still pursue our hearts. This is certainly expressed in the poem, the "Hound of Heaven" written at the on set of the century by Francis Thompson.

> I fled Him, down the nights and down the days;
>   I fled Him, down the arches of the years;
> I fled Him, down the labyrinthine ways
>   Of my own mind; and in the mist of tears
> I hid from Him, and under running laughter;
>   Up vistaed hopes I sped;
>   And shot, precipitated,
>   Adown Titanic glooms of chasmed fears,
> From those strong Feet that followed, followed after.
>   But with unhurrying chase,
>   And unperturbed pace,
> Deliberate speed, majestic instancy,
>   They beat — and a Voice beat

More instant than the Feet—
"All things betray thee, who betrayest Me."

This element of being sought after by a Master is what connects
all of us who hunger and thirst. It is like a rod that will guide us in
our 'coming home' that we may not get lost. And even if the desert
may seem barren, we shall not die thirsty in our walking.

I realized that this was clearly my story. For many times in
the past, I became so hungry with the material world. I had been so
focused on what is ephemeral and temporal. I had been so engrossed
with filling a certain need which is not an essential one in this life.
But as events unfolded, God pursued me and let me feel that He was
at my side. That He will stay with me and never leave me.

He Knows my Name

When I hear the passage about the Good Shepherd, I find it hard to put myself into the scene. First, that parable was inspired by a scene in the culture of Jesus' time and place. Secondly, I seldom see sheep. In the few times I visited our local zoo, I just saw a flock of sheep. A rabble of wool. A mount of cotton. A herd of hooves. That's it. Everything seems the same. Everything is flat. All of them are white---dirty white.

But not so with the Shepherd. To him, every sheep is different. Every face is special. Every face has a story. And every sheep has a name. The one with the scar on the feet, that's Daphne. And the fellow with one ear dangling and one ear erect, I call him Eden. And the small one with the black patch on his leg, he's an orphan with no brothers. I call him Star. He knows each and everyone of them.

The Shepherd knows his sheep. He calls them by name.

When we see people, we see a multitude, a bunch of human beings. We see people, not persons, but people. A herd of creatures. A flock of individuals. That's how we view them.

It is not true with the Shepherd. To him, every face has a different message to convey. Every face tells a story. Every face is a child. Every child has a name. The one with the weary eyes and bruises on his body, that's Itok. The old fellow with a mole on his chin, Emong is his name. And the young one with the limp? He's an orphan with no brothers. I call him Michael. The one with dirty feet, that's Nené. He knows each one deep within.

Even if the sheep are preoccupied with their own hunger, The Shepherd looks kindly at them. He will never abandon them because

90

he knows each one by name. The Shepherd knows you. He knows your name. And he will never forget it.

"I have written your name on my hand" (Isaiah 49:16)

Quite an assurance to ponder upon, isn't it? Your name carved on God's hand. Your name on God's lips. Perhaps we see our names on the graffiti, on the walls; or from a magazine, or from a sticker. Maybe you've seen your name in some special places. Or maybe you've heard your name on TV—an advertisement, a game show, or a reality TV show. But to think that your name is on God's hand and on God's lips--- It is as certain as the dawn.

God looks lovingly at us even if we are so busy eating. In the times we center our concern on ourselves, God caresses our backs and tells us, "Eat heartily my son." And He would whisper and call us by our names. He will pursue us no matter what, no matter when.

Fullness of Life

Jesus' concern is not just to save souls, but to bring us all of life's blessings. Our aim in life is not just to go to heaven but to help bring about the new heaven and the new earth which means it is about real life blessings. It is not just the "when-you-die-you-go-to-paradise mentality." It is the blessing here and now. When Jesus said that He came to bring good news to the poor, it literally means food for the hungry, houses for the homeless, health for the sick, freedom for the oppressed, sight to the blind. This is not just symbolic.

"May your roots go down deep into the soil of God's marvelous love. And may you have the power to understand, as all God's people should, how wide, how long, how high, and how deep His love really is. May you experience the love of Christ, though it is so great you will never fully understand it. Then you will be filled with the fullness of life and power

91

that comes from God."

(Ephesians 3:17-19)

I believe this is the real mission of the Shepherd. I grew up believing like the majority of Christians, that what matters most is salvation of souls and all else are unimportant because God alone is enough and all things are passing. This is true but incomplete. Jesus came to give us fullness of life and this fullness is NOW and it is not just about churchy concepts. It is about tangible material blessings for all people such as food and decent living conditions. Though He desires to bring us to enjoy eternal life in heaven, He also makes us see that He can bring forth the kingdom of God onto the dilapidated table made of scrap wooden crates with the rusty drums and the worn out tires. I am awakened to a new perspective in terms of what the theologians mean when they say Church of the Poor. There is no such thing as spiritual and non-spiritual actions if the Spirit of God is present. We cannot dichotomize the spirit of God. If His Spirit is around, even the non-spiritual non-Church activities are spiritual. That is the reason why social issues are so spiritual. *

These were the issues of concern before the Shepherd was slaughtered; before He died a poor man's death. These issues were also the reason why He was killed. How interesting it is that Jesus came not only to bring souls to heaven, but to give the good news of complete and total well-being for all His people and creation. The scope is very wide. It covers as wide as from the needs of his sheep to even the ecology and care for nature. We are all part of the good news He is talking about...in our own small way, wherever we are. This is the Biblical Jesus. This is the Shepherd I want to follow and to know. Not only the Jesus that was taught to us in the Western Tradition...Who is often the all-forgiving Lord of our miserable sins. He covers far and

---

* Carlos Abesamis, a priest who has spent his life exploring spirituality and has written many books about the Biblical Jesus, makes an interesting observation. His main thesis is that Jesus did not come just to save souls but to bring us all of life's blessings. Our aim ni life in not just to go to heaven but to help bring about the new heavens and the new earth. It means real life blessings.

92

wide. His mercy is a given. He gave his life not only for our eternal salvation. He is so big a God that the salvific mission includes giving us a life which is according to His very plan. It's not just a foretaste of life but "fullness of life," which is possible here on earth if everyone at the table of our Savior has the consciousness of the importance of social justice which is in the essence of man. Each participant at the table is called to be part of this "life-giving" journey.

Are we life-giving to the person next to us?..even if he does not pay attention to us? Am I a living presence to people, to my family, to my neighbors, to my co-workers? Do I assure them of peace when I am around? Or do I bring them discord?

Christ invited these poor children to the table to show them that He is not a distant hard-to-reach God but a very near one. He proves that He does not talk to them from afar but 'up close and personal.' The rejected and down trodden are his priority. Not the loud and the rich who feast out of people's misery. Jesus fills up these poor children's cups because His love is overflowing.

I have learned many things in my experience with the Hapag children. But nothing else is as important as knowing that God's love is unlimited and unconditional—that we are truly loved—right here, right now, just the way we are. I would like to share this beautiful passage from the back cover of the book "What's So Amazing About Grace?" by Philip Yancy, a Baptist.

THERE IS NOTHING WE CAN DO FOR
GOD TO LOVE US MORE.

THERE IS NOTHING WE CAN DO FOR
GOD TO LOVE US LESS.

How beautiful. I stopped when I read this passage and stayed with it for days. Think about this....there is nothing you can do for God to love you more. You are already loved. To the full. No amount of spiritual calisthenics and renunciations, no amount of knowledge gained from readings, no amount of crusading on behalf of righteous causes. There is nothing you can do for Him to lessen that love. No sin will change His mind about us. No sin. Nothing. God's love for us is beyond what we can or cannot do. It is UNEARNED. It is called GRACE. Pure grace.

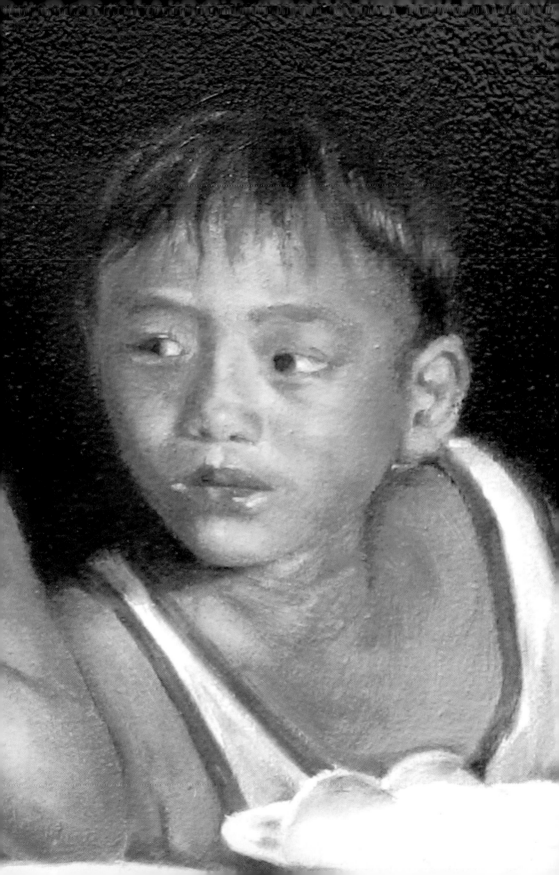

THEY HAVE JESUS

CHAPTER 6

The Hunger of Onse

I saw this 10-year-old boy in Litex. Kids and adults call him "Onse," not only because his real name was Leoncio but because he always had those two lines of viscous, slippery greenish mucous substance that race their way from both holes of his nose down to the edge of his upper lip. The gummy worm-like fluid forms the figure of eleven that is why they named him "Onse" (The Spanish for number eleven). With his tongue pointed upwards, it would leak the dense fluid like an erratic wiper of a windshield. He would casually swipe it with his right arm and wipe it anywhere he wanted it to be, whether on the wall or on his fellow kids. Onse was the second child of four. The eldest was his mom's son to a first husband. His mother recently prepared to fly for work in Japan but this plan did not push through. His father works as an assistant *"pahinante"* [porter]to a truck driver who hauls gravel and sand. Their youngest son was sold for P3,000 to a childless couple whose business activity is "five-six" [loaning to others at very high interest rates]. In spite of their poverty, his father is hooked on all sorts of drugs from rugby to shabu. *"Humihingi po s'ya lagi ng pera kay mama dahil gusto daw po n'ya umi-score."* [He's always asking Mom for money for his vices.] He declared in a naïve manner.

Swallowing Shame

Onse is the laughing stock of the other kids and even of adults. They make fun of him when he speaks because he stutters. His ways and gestures amuse people too. Unfortunately, they mock him about his parents, mainly his mother who works in the club as a strip dancer and singer. Mariz, a petite but rather sexy young mother, had three more sisters who worked in the bar as entertainers too. Aling Binay, their own mother, traded them when they were in their teens. According to Jinggo, their neighbor and childhood chum, Mariz would striptease in front of them when they were younger while drinking gin at a nearby corner. Her present husband was even with them then, cheering and getting wild, until Mariz got pregnant for the second time. *"Kaya naman pong sikmurain ni Onad 'yun e. Matibay naman po ang bituka noong taong 'yon."* [Onad, the husband, can take it anyway. He's made of stern stuff.] For almost ten years until after she was living with her husband, she worked on and off in different bars particularly at Crystal Ice and Catherine Club. At present, her own husband is the one trading her.

"Sport lang po ang tatay niyan," [His dad is sport] the shirtless

98

street thug Jinggo recounts.

"Ba't mo naman nasabi?" [What made you say that?] I asked...

"Dahil ok lang po sa kanya na sumayaw yung misis n'ya sa club at magpapa "table" sa customer...siyempre po may kita s'ya at pambili ng droga" [Because it's okay with him that his wife dances and entertains customers… this way, he'd have earnings and money to buy drugs.] And he demonstrates how Mariz dances seductively all the way. *"Kahit nga po naglalakad dito 'yong Nanay n'yan na maikli ang mini-skirt ok lang kahit sipulan ng mga lasing e."* [It's okay for him even if Onse's mom, his wife, walks in a mini-skirt, even while drunkards whistle at her.]

I looked at the face of Onse and there was sadness and gloom. He is so young but he seems to feel and understand.

He was 9 years old when he posed for the Hapag. Since then, he hasn't tried entering any school.

"*Wala po kasi akong birth certificate kaya 'di ako makapag-aral....* [I don't have a birth certificate so I can't go to school…]

"*Gusto ko maging duktor para matulungan 'yong mga tao*" [I want to be a doctor so I can help people] Onse said with confidence. I gestured that we move near the parked trycicle under the shaded spot.

"*Sa Litex po ako nakatira... sa amin po 'yong pinakamalaking bahay sa squatter.*" [I live in Litex, ours is the biggest house in the squatters' area.]

"*So mayaman pala kayo?*" [So, you must be rich?] I smilingly verified.

"*Hindi po...May kaya lang po.*" [No, we can just afford more.]

I really couldn't help but laugh at his natural way of responding to questions.
"*Ikaw ba ang panganay?*" [Are you the eldest?]
"*Hindi po... May kuya po ako sa stepfather. May asawa po noong una 'yong nanay ko. 'Yong kapatid kong bunso binenta po. Tatlong libo.*" [No, I have an older brother from my stepfather. My mom had a first husband. My youngest sibling was sold for P3,000.]

"Nag-aaral ka ba?" [Do you study?]

"Anong trabaho ni Itay mo?" [What's your dad's work?]

"Nagbubuhat po ng bagaheng malalaki ang tatay ko." [He carries heavy baggages.]

"Mama ko sa bahay lang. Alas dose na po ng tanghali nagigising e." [My mom only stays at home. She regularly wakes up 12:00 noon.]

"Madalas ka ba mapagalitan?" [Are you often scolded?]

"Pinapalo po ako." [I am often spanked.]

"Ano ang pinangpapalo sa iyo 'pag may kasalanan ka... bakal?" [What do they use to spank you when you have done something wrong...a steel bar?]

"Naku hindi po. Tubo po." [No. A pipe.]

"E' di ba bakal nga 'yong tubo?" [A pipe is made of steel, isn't it?]

"Hindi po. Plastic...." [No. It's made of plastic...] He corrected me as though he was older than I.

"Ahh... plastic....ah meron nga namang ganoon. 'Yong... na bebend. Anong kulay 'yon?" [Ahh...plastic...there are pipes made of plastic. The ones that can be bent. What is the color of the pipe?]

101

"PVC blue."

"Ahh... PVC Blue....masakit din 'yon ah" [Ahh…PVC Blue… that also hurts.] I realized while scratching my head.

"Mahal ba tayo ni Jesus?" [Does Jesus love us?] I asked this question while showing him my painting's printed copy. He was the one in sando shirt with blue lining.

"Opo." [Yes]

"Paano mo nalamang mahal tayo ni Jesus?" [How did you know that He loves us?]

"Dahil po Siya ang May gawa sa atin eh." [Because He was the One Who made us.]

"Tatay po natin Siya eh. Mga anak po tayo ni Hesus. Kaya N'ya po tayo mahal eh. Pumunta po akong Quiapo at nakita ko po si Jesus nakapako. Sabi ko kung sino man may gawa n'yan paparusahan po sila." [He is our Father. We are the children of Jesus. That's why He loves us. I went to Quiapo and I saw Jesus crucified. I said whoever did that will definitely be punished.]

"Anong gagawin mo?" [What will you do?]

"Pipigilan ko po sila." [I will stop them.]

"Ipagtatanggol ko po S'ya." [I will defend Him.]

"Paano mo ipagtatanggol? Anong gagawin mo sa mga sundalo?"
[How will you defend Him? What will you do to the soldiers?]

"Sumpak na maliit ang gagamitin ko sa kanila." [I will use a small popgun on them]

"Si Jesus po nagbuhay sa kanila tapos gaganoonin lang nila." [Jesus gave them life, then why will they do that to Him?]

"Mabait ka ba Onse? Sumusunod ka ba sa mga utos ng magulang mo?" [Are you good Onse? Do you follow your parent's orders?]

"Noong nakulong po si papa ko sa Singko, lagi po akong pumupun-ta kay papa eh. Naglalakad lang ako. Napagbintangan s'ya na nagsnatch ng cellphone . May sarili naman po s'yang cellphone. Dinamay lang s'ya ng kabarkada n'ya eh. Kaya ayaw ko pong magbarkada eh. Gusto ko pong barkada 'yong di umiinom, hindi nagbibisyo. Dalawang linggo rin s'yang nakulong."

[When my papa was imprisoned in Singko, I would always visit him. I would just walk to the jail. He was accused of snatching a cellular phone. But he has his own. He was just implicated by his friends. That's why I don't want to be involved in gangs eh. I'd like to have friends who don't drink, who have no vices. Papa was in jail for two weeks]

"Minsan nagigipit din po kami eh." [Sometimes we are short of money]

"Tatlo ang mga TV namin eh. 'Yong dalawa di gumagana. 'Yong isa binenta. Madaling araw nangangalakal po kami ng lolo ko. Lolo ko po si Piyô."

[We had three television sets. Two of those don't work. We

sold the other one. My grandfather and I start work very early in the morning. Tisyo is my grandfather]

"Ahh...lolo mo pala 'yong matandang may bukol sa ulo?" [Ahh... so your grandfather is the old man with a bump on his head?] referring to a male model I hired for another painting.

"Hindi po. Tatlo lang po ang buhok noon eh." [No. He only has three strands of hair eh]

"Kuwento ka pa...." [Tell me more stories...]

"Pinsan ko nakulong. Nagnakaw po kasi ng mga pantalon sa sampayan. Sabi ko 'wag na magnakaw, mangalakal na lang sila eh pero 'di pa rin sila sumunod eh. Tara kuya bibigyan na lang kita ng pera sa ipon ko 'wag ka lang magnanakaw. D'yan marami ka pang kikitain. Gipit na nga kayo saka ka pa magnanakaw."
[My cousin was jailed. He stole pairs of pants hanging on the clothesline. I told him not to steal and to work instead, but he did not follow my advice. I told him I'd give him money from my savings just so that he wouldn't steal. I said he'd earn much from working and that stealing would only aggravate the situation.]

He recited his prayer with folded hands.
"Jesus, thank You po sa lahat ng binigay Mong mga biyaya at thank You din po sa mga ginawa N'yo sa tao. Sana po maging duktor ako balang araw." [Jesus, thank You for all the blessings You have given me and thank You for the things You've done for people. I hope I can become a doctor someday.]

I also asked Onse if he feels loved by people and friends.

He complained that he was always being ridiculed by people. When he joins the group in junk hunting, he feels insecure because he was once chased and bitten by two dogs on his buttocks. According to him, it was so painful that he wasn't able to go out of the house for more than two weeks.

"...*pinapahabol po ako sa aso noong may-ari ng bahay. Nakadapa na nga po ako kinakagat pa' ko eh.*" [The owner of the house lets his dog chase me. Sometimes, I've already fallen down, the dog still bites me.]

When they go from house to house, people would always look down at them with suspicion. "*Maliit at mababa po ang tingin ng mga tao sa amin lalo na 'yong mga mayayaman. Mayabang po sila.*" [People belittle us, the rich especially. They are haughty.] At his age, he feels the torment of not being trusted by others. They even hurt him in the head a couple of times. "*Maraming beses na po ako nakutosan ng matatanda. Binabato pa nga po nila ako 'pag nakakailag ako sa batok.*" [The old people have rapped me on the head many times. When I'm able to dodge, they throw stones at me.]

From Onse, another unfolding light that humbled me as much as it awed me was a reminder of the meaning of Jesus' poverty: not to be taken seriously, to be valued like a rag. The poor are very much like that. The Book of Sirach has this to say:

"If the rich person slips, many come to the rescue;
    he speaks unseemly words, but they justify him.
If the humble person slips, they even criticize him;
    he talks sense, but is not given a hearing.

The rich person speaks and all are silent;
> they extol to the clouds what he says.
The poor person speaks and they say, 'Who is this fellow?'
> And should he stumble, they even push him down.."
>> (Sirach 13: 22-23)

The Poor Artist

It is indeed a humbling experience to be taken for granted and to be doubted by others. Yes, we do need money; we need material resources, too, to keep us moving.

The world of Fine Arts is a totally different world to me. In my interest to widen my knowledge and to gain more ideas and styles in the field, I became a member of the Arts Association of the Philippines, the hub of both veteran as well as budding artists of our time. Because I frequented our center and mingled with these people, my eyes witnessed the sad plight of the Filipino artists. Other countries respect and give high regard to people of the arts. It is not so in our country. The famous ones, including the National Artists, are but a speck in the industry. They are just the tip of the iceberg, so to say. Underneath the waters are the countless poor and unrecognized but nonetheless very good artists ---perhaps far better than those who were acclaimed to great heights. These struggling fellow artists were often belittled and trampled upon. I saw with my very eyes how they were degraded and exploited by galleries and rich patrons. One of the warmest and amiable people in our country is the artist. Some are *"utu-uto"* (easy to persuade) because it is easy to bargain and haggle prices with them. He is a very easy-to-please individual. He does marvelous works but he has simple joys.

The collectors would allure them and take advantage of their hunger for money. These artists can't even buy complete sets of materials. They can't even mount their canvasses on easels. They live in the slums and in the squatter areas. They grow old and die without experiencing solo exhibits. At times, they have to loan their works at very meager amounts only to have them forfeited in the end.

I encountered a very good artist from the south. He was so good in verdaccio, my favorite technique. When he had his first art show, he was already 55 years old. Promotions, prints, invitations, media write-ups, press releases and television exposures were made. I attended the event and saw how saleable his works were even if those thirty or so paintings cost P100,000 each. Roughly in my estimate, he garnered a neat P3 million that night because almost all were sold. When I talked to him and congratulated him for his healthy profit, he intimated to me that he was only given P5,000 by the gallery sponsor for his appearance. He said that the paintings were no longer his property because they were forfeited by the sponsor a long time ago for P3,000 – P5,000 each. The poor are not mere abstractions or statistics. They are real people.

Such is the degrading plight of the artists in our time. They reflect, too, the poverty in society. I could not have learned this aspect of poverty if I did not immerse in their situation. I too helped the poor - but more on a one time first-and-last basis. Yes, to be poor is not just to be without, but more so, not to be treated seriously. Is this not what Christianity means? The cross was not only a symbol of torture but more so a symbol of non-importance. Only the non-important and the despicable are sent to the cross. To follow Jesus also means to be taken as not significant.

How many times have I encountered humbling questions like, *"Artist ka pala? Pakigawa naman 'yong project ng anak kong grade 3"* or *"Pakidrawing naman sa coupon bond 'yong nililigawan kong chick."* ["So, you're an artist? Could you please make the project of my child who is in grade 3" or "Could you please draw a figure of the girl I'm courting on a piece of coupon bond?"]

Wittingly or sometimes unwittingly, people would ask, "What are you painting that for? Don't you think it is such a waste of time?"

"What are you writing that book for?...You are a business person, you are a wood trader, what will you write about?" "Will we earn money from that?" "Why do you gather these kids? Aren't you just taking them for a ride?" "They might know where you live and beg you for more money."

We need to be constantly reminded that in life, it is not always important to be in the best place of the table. At times, we need to undergo the humbling experience of Christ; with the feelings of the poor when they are looked down upon. To be a Christian is to share in the non-importance of the Crucified.

St. Francis of Assissi explained to Brother Leo:

"When we come to St. Mary of the Angels, soaked
by the rain and frozen by the cold, all soiled with mud
and suffering from hunger, and we ring at the gate of
the Place and the brother porter comes and says angrily:

'Who are you?' And we say: 'We are two of your brothers.' And he contradicts us, saying: 'You are not telling
the truth. Rather you are two rascals who go around
deceiving people and stealing what they give to the
poor. Go away.' And he does not open for us, but makes
us stand outside in the snow and rain, cold and hungry,
until night falls-then if we endure all those insults and
cruel rebuffs patiently, without being troubled and without complaining, and if we reflect humbly and charita-
bly that that porter really knows us and that God makes
him speak against us, oh, Brother Leo, write that perfect
joy is there!

And if we continue to knock, and the porter
comes out in anger, and drives us away with curses and
hard blows like bothersome scoundrels, saying; 'Get
away from here, you dirty thieves-go to the hospital!
Who do you think you are? You certainly won't eat
or sleep here'--and if we bear it patiently and take the
insults with joy and love in our hearts, Oh, Brother Leo,
write that that is perfect joy!

And if later, suffering intensely from hunger and
the painful cold, with night falling, we still knock and
call, and crying loudly beg them to open for us and let
us come in for the love of God, and he grows still more
angry and says: 'Those fellows are bold and shame-
less ruffians. I'll give them what they deserve.' And he
comes out with a knotty club, and grasping us by the
cowl throws us onto the ground, rolling us in the mud
and snow, and beats us with that club so much that
he covers our bodies with wounds--if we endure all
those evils and insults and blows with joy and patience,

reflecting that we must accept and bear the sufferings of the Blessed Christ patiently for love of Him, oh, Brother Leo, write that: that is perfect joy!

And now hear the conclusion, Brother Leo. Above all the graces and gifts of the Holy Spirit which Christ gives to His friends is that of conquering oneself and willingly enduring sufferings, insults, humiliations, and hardships for the love of Christ. For we cannot glory in all those other marvelous gifts of God, as they are not ours but God's, as the Apostle says: 'What have you that you have not received?' But we can glory in the cross of tribulations and afflictions, because that is ours, and so the Apostle says: 'I will not glory save in the Cross of Our Lord Jesus Christ.'" (Fioretti di San Francesco)

The sacrifice of Jesus on the cross is so significant for the whole cosmos. It is the center of salvation history. It changed the destiny of the whole human race, yet when Jesus hanged on the cross people did not even dignify him by paying attention to him. He was just one of those malefactors who did stupid things. The fourth Servant Song of Isaiah puts it:

"He was despised, the lowest of men... one from whom, as it were, we averted our gaze, despised, for whom we had no regard"

(Is 53,3)

Legacy

As of this writing, I feel so hesitant and afraid. I fear that when my small kids grow up and have the chance to read these thoughts, they might just get the wrong signal and focus on poverty and not become successful financially as I have dreamed of them to be. I honestly worry about this. They might not be attracted to the business arena. However, when I look at the eyes of Onse, I ask myself, do I really take the poor people seriously? Is my charity more of a "good riddance attitude?" At times I would like to think that to dole out money in charity is one of the easiest and more gratifying things especially when you have more in life. You sprinkle fractions from your window where you lay resting on your cushion, feeling the cool breath of your aircon---and people applaud... and praise you because it is a big amount for them. For you, it is just a pittance. A "Cushion Charity." It is like igniting a bamboo cannon on a New Year's eve. You put fire on the small hole, cover your ears, and hurriedly dash away... afraid...to get near the fire.

....afraid to get involved...

The hardest is to get involved. To expose oneself. One cannot say I love God if he doesn't get under the skin of the poor...

I would like to address this to my own children:

I truly desire and dream of you to be high achievers of our society someday, to be financially independent, to be successful in a chosen career or enterprise....but all these are nothing if your life is not shared with others, especially the poor. This is the legacy I want to hand down to you and the children of your children. It is only at this point in my life that I understand with clarity what my Mom used to remind me of and whisper to my ear before I embarked on every new endeavor: "Life will only be MEANINGFUL if and when it is shared with others."

In the same light, I want to apologize for the times I missed out in showing kindness to people. For the times I did not set the right example to my kids. How may I ever make up for that? For the other similar things I missed out, I am sorry! Please allow me to make up! Let us spend more time while we are together in this world with the poor.

"So many people walk around with a meaningless life. They seem half-asleep, even when they're busy doing things they think are important. This is because they're chasing the wrong things. The way you get meaning into your life is to devote yourself to loving others, devote yourself to your community around you, and devote yourself to creating something that gives you purpose and meaning."

Morrie Schwartz (the book "Tuesdays with Morrie")

THEY HAVE JESUS

CHAPTER 7

Crumbs of a Child

Old men ought to be explorers
Here or there does not matter
We must be still and still moving
Into another intensity
For a further union, a deeper communion
Through the dark cold and the empty desolation,
The wave cry, the wind cry, the vast waters
Of the petrel and the porpoise. In my end is my beginning.
(T.S. Eliot, "East Coker")

I am writing this chapter not with ink but with my own blood. I say so because the skinny child under the table who eats with the cat is not a street child from any area of the Metropolis. He is not a child living in the gutter or sewerage. He is not the hungry kid who roams in our busy streets at night. He is not one of those who shiver in the dark and wake up with nightmares in daytime when monsters are real.

The child under the table is none other than ME.

Yes, he is the symbol of a desperate person eating the crumbs and crawling his way towards the light. For so many years now, I was a resentful hesitant child who preferred to stay underneath....than to join the rest of the children eating with Jesus. For so many years, too, I had been groping in the dark abyss. I was drawn to a different light. My eyes had been fixed on what glittered and sparkled momentarily only to witness them getting extinguished at an instant.

Ironically, the small child is an imaginary symbolic figure of a man- a man, who in the years that passed, had satisfied himself with unnecessary food but felt a different hunger in the end; a man who filled himself with so much pleasure only to find himself under the table eating the spiritual crumbs and crawling towards the light.

"Late have I loved you, O Beauty ever ancient,
ever new, late have I loved you! You were within me,
but I was outside, and it was there that I searched
for you. In my unloveliness I plunged into the lovely
things which you created. You were with me, but I
was not with you. Created things kept me from you;
yet if they had not been in you they would have not
been at all. You called, you shouted, and you broke
through my deafness. You flashed, you shone, and you

dispelled my blindness. You breathed your fragrance
on me; I drew in breath and now I pant for you. I
have tasted you, now I hunger and thirst for more.
You touched me, and I burned for your peace."
(from the "Confessions of Saint Augustine")

The Unknown Sudan Boy

The model reference I used for this child was the 'Pulitzer Prize'-
winning photo taken in 1994 during the Sudan Famine. The picture
shows a heart-breaking scene of a starving child who collapsed on the
ground, struggling to get to a food center in Sudan, Africa in 1993.
In the background, a vulture stalks the emaciated child. The vulture
is waiting for the child to die so that it can eat the tiny human being.
No one knows what happened to the child, including the photogra-

pher himself- Kevin Carter who left the place afterwards.

Three months later, Carter was found dead of carbon-monoxide poisoning in Johannesburg, a suicide at 33. His red pick-up truck was parked near a small river where he used to play as a child; a green garden hose attached to the vehicle's exhaust funneled the fumes inside. "I'm really, really sorry," he explained in a note left on the passenger seat beneath a knapsack. "The pain of life overrides the joy to the point that joy does not exist." He killed himself due to depression. The note he left behind was a litany of nightmares and dark visions, a clutching attempt at autobiography, self-analysis, explanation, excuse... "I am haunted by the vivid memories of killings & corpses; anger & pain...of starving or wounded children, of trigger-happy madmen, often police, of killer executioners..."

Sudan Kid, Kevin and I

There was one thing in common among the three of us (Kevin Carter, the boy, and I). All three of us crawled our way in an attempt to reach for something worth our journey. Kevin did not reach the finish line because he quit and ended his life. The future was bleak and he decided to end his life. The boy's inch-by-inch crawl towards food was really vague and uncertain. No one knew whether he reached the supply camp or not. Like an infantryman in battle, I crawled with a heavy gear, exhausted, struggling, and was eager to get myself out of a foxhole after seeking cover from enemy fire, and finally reached for the light.

I crawled towards the wrong light.

The past years have been frenetic and productive especially in business. I was a multi- tasker of sorts. My desire was always to do something grand. Or so I thought. I did what I thought pleased people. I worked on so many projects all at the same time. I was a busy man. After each task, I would dust off my hand a bit and would feel as energetic as when I started. I never wanted to pause before plunging myself into the next conquest; always on the go. I worked like crazy. I struggled to prove myself. I poured my best efforts and talents, but in the end, things fell apart for me.

I was diagnosed with an illness and the world stopped revolving. It stopped in the sphere where the sun was hidden and there was total darkness.

My Faith was under Fire

Over the past two years, the journey has been, and still is, rather rough for me. Caught up in the demands of a midlife transition, after giving what I thought was my best to my family and work, to the clients that patronize us, a series of events precipitated my own personal experience of a long and bewildering descent into darkness. All these, and more, have made me scamper around trying to find answers to questions, the likes of which I have never encountered before.

I begin to wonder why such a very energetic man like myself, seemingly invincible and strong, in his prime had to be confined… with bottled water on the right hand and a urinal on the left… in the four walls of a hospital room on a regular basis and at the mercy of doctors and nurses.

Why did I get sick?

This question baffled me. But I now accept and embrace the vagueness of it all. I am beginning to know in my heart that life's meaning and goal is beyond the events that seemingly shatters our life. To give answers to my endless questions is definitely not part of my crawl.

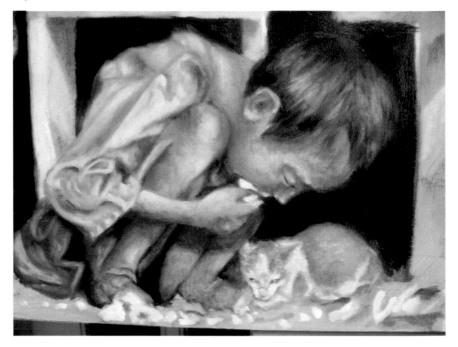

"If knowing the answers to life's questions is absolutely necessary to you, then forget the journey. You will never make it, for this is a journey of unknowables---of unanswered questions, enigmas, incomprehensibles, and most of all, things unfair."

-Madame Jean Guyon

Those words struck me like a bullet and have stayed lodged inside me. This realization was like an unfolding light that humbled me as much as it awed me.

"God does all these things to a man—twice, even three times—to turn back his soul from the pit, that the light of life may shine on him."
Job 33:29

The Broken Last Supper

In the latter part of 2004, a year before I painted the Hapag, I was in the midst of a terrible crisis in my life. Literally, I was in darkness. I felt so confused about a physical and chronic discomfort I was experiencing in my stomach…in my whole being. I went to several hospitals and doctors including psychiatrists. I approached several counselors, both priests and lay, but found no answers. I lost weight and I became a recluse. I was inside a very deep and dim well, eager to get out even if it took climbing while clasping a rope filled with thorns and broken glass.

In one of my most desperate moments one day after Christmas, I went to an *"manggagamot"* (quack doctor). He had a small chapel built under the patronage of San Martin De Pores. All the statues of saints and heroes you can think of, including Rizal, were enthroned all over the small sanctuary. There were country folks who looked like fanatics kneeling down and prostrating before the altar. Funny, but Ka Martin literally resembled the face of his black patron saint:

121

curly hair…dark skin…African nose. He had a silver metal on one of his teeth that glittered while he smiled. He shampooed my hair with authentic coconut oil which was a bit repugnant. Puffing a brown cigar, he looked at me with weary poodle eyes and asked, *"Ano ba ang kinakatakot mo?"* [What are you afraid of?]

"Kamatayan…" I softly said. [Death]

"Masyado kang duwag. Kung mamamatay ka na, hindi ka maka-kapasok sa loob ng kapilyang ito. Hanggang hagdan ka lang at tutumba ka." [You're such a coward. If you're about to die, you won't be able even to enter this chapel. You'll only reach the stairs and you'll fall.]

I looked at him with a poker face.

He intimated to me that he does not receive payments and he boasted that the chapel was built out of the contributions of his patients.

He suggested, *"Alam mo iho…. dapat mag deboto ka kay San Antonio."* [You know son…you should become a devotee of St. Anthony.]

My mother butted in with what she considered a question-able advice. " *'Di ba patron saint s'ya ng mga nawawala?"* (Isn't he the patron saint of the lost?)

We were surprised with the wisdom of Ka Martin when he declared, *"Tama! 'Di ba nawawala ka sa sarili?…."* (Right! Aren't you losing yourself?)

We laughed but we realized he was right.

He got a small basin half filled with lukewarm water. While dropping melted candle wax, the quacky shook his head in utter disgust with what he saw with the multi-figure that formed and said,

"Kaya pala sumasakit 'yang tiyan mo eh. May pinabayaan kang rebulto. Hanapin mo! Bigyan mo ng pagkain. Busugin mo." [Now I know why your stomach is aching. You have a statue that is quite neglected. Look for it! Give it food.]

I was so skeptical but I remembered two years earlier when I bought a table top Last Supper figurine from Italy which I mutilated and whose bread, chalice, and plates I grinded in view of modifying them with details. That's what I usually do when developing and improving a product. With the turn of events, I forgot all about the unfinished piece and junked it in a stock room adjacent to the resin area of my factory.

"Opo. Tama ka, Ka Martin." I confessed. *"May naaalala nga ako na ganoon."* [Yes, You're right, Ka Martin. I do remember such a thing.]

He blessed me and said, *"Humayo ka at busugin ang ginutom mo..."* [Go and feed that which you left hungry.]

We were like fools. I hurriedly dropped a P500-bill into the donation box and rushed to my shop to look for that abandoned piece. I removed the thick dust, frantically got small improvised plates and filled them with real rice and sprayed them with hardener. Mighty bond…retouch paints…accent of gold, etc. I put small pieces of fruits and woof! Suddenly, there was a feast in that empty table. It was crazy of me to ride on with the quack doctor's idea and pay heed to his advice, but I was really so desperate.

When I got home, I felt rejuvenated but not back to my former energy. Until this present day, the restored Last Supper figurine is displayed prominently in our house. Not long after that, I was diagnosed with my real physical illness and eventually was operated on in January of 2005. I forgot all about that controversial figurine…

While convalescing, I crawled towards a canvas and grabbed a brush. I wanted to be productive. The urge to paint seized me. The need to be needed set in. I dabbled into portraits both in oil and acrylic. I started with an obra of Our Lady of Mediatrix, a dream vision I saw twice in split second before my operation. When almost all our walls had been filled like a gallery, I noticed that there was an empty wall that had to be filled---the dining room. It was quite big so I prepared a large canvass and imagined putting still life with hyper-realistic native fruits with the likes of guyabano and rambutan. When we were eating as a family, I realized that my kids had become quite choosy with food and that they had much left-over. "There are many hungry children out there and even all over the world who are suffering," I always told them. I noticed that my words were powerless and empty, so I thought of painting a Last Supper situated in the slums to make the hunger vividly poignant.

Not long after the painting was mounted on our wall, people came to our house and the story has spread around. They were saying that it has reached many hearts and has healed many lives. This is a great blessing from God.

The completion of the Hapag painting happened almost exactly
a year after that fateful visit to Ka Martin in San Rafael, Bulacan...
a year after drops of candle wax merged and formed many figures of
hungry people who gathered around a long table...a year after the
albularyo scolded me and said: *"Kaya pala sumasakit yang tiyan mo
eh. May ginutom kang rebulto. Hanapin mo! Bigyan mo ng pagkain.
Busugin mo."* [So that was the reason why your stomach was aching.
You forgot about a statue. Look for it! Give it food.]

I can't help but look back at that strange moment because I
realized that God could have used simple people whom I sometimes
belittle, not necessarily to cure me physically, but to shed some light
in my grim and gloomy days. I could not help but smile upon thinking of the silver highlight on his tooth and the old faded plastic basin
where the candle floated. God can also reveal some rays of wisdom
through its ripples.

True enough, there were real hungry apostles waiting for me...
and these apostles were the poor children who were given life and
hope in my painting.

A Drifter Crawling towards Pilgrimhood

There is so much pain in remembering those days when it
seemed I would crack beneath the pressure. The words in the Bible
were foreign to me at that time. All of these jolted my faith in God
and I am still trying to pick up the pieces of a long nightmare. Yes,
my own faith had been shaken in recent years, especially after this

illness that almost killed me and still threatens me. I cried out to God for help, and it's hard to know just how He answers. Really, can we count on God, I asked? There had always been this archaic belief in me that I had to prove my worth to God. My concept of a God was an authority figure to whom I needed to prove myself to gain a little piece of heaven in the end. I thought that if I was not good, He would abandon me. All along, though I was unaware of it, He was just walking at my side.

"God gives us just enough to seek Him, and never enough to fully find Him. To do more would inhibit our freedom, and our freedom is very dear to God."

-Ron Hansen

Still I had a kind of baseline confidence in God. Though it may have seemed deluded, I believed at a very deep level that God was in control. Some people call that having a crutch. I called it my faith. For a crippled person, there is one thing worse than having a crutch, after all---having no crutch.

"You do not want to leave too, do you?" Jesus asked his disciples in a tone somewhere between plaintiveness and resignation.

I said with Peter, "Lord, to whom shall we go?"

Digging deep into my inner resources really meant poring through the best that my spiritual storehouse could muster. Fortunate enough to have found the right space and time to reflect, a powerful realization slowly dawned on me.

The prophet Jeremiah writes of a bush that sets its roots on parched desert soil. In times of rainfall and prosperity the plant flourishes, but during drought its shallow roots shrivel and die. Jeremiah draws a contrast with the one who lives in faith:

> "...blessed is the man who trusts in the Lord,
> whose confidence is in Him.
> He will be like a tree planted by the water
> That sends out its roots by the stream.
> It does not fear when heat comes;
> Its leaves are always green.
> It has no worries in a year of drought
> And never fails to bear fruit."

The Lord makes no rosy promises about living only in springtime. Instead, He points toward faith that helps us prepare for arid seasons. Harsh winters will come, followed by scorching summers. Yet if the roots of faith go deep enough, tapping into Living Water, we can survive the drought times and flourish in times of plenty.

These words reflect succinctly this paradoxical situation of healthy tension that best describes the life of a pilgrim like me. Ironically, the experience of the dark brought me to the gradual appreciation of the light that was slowly dawning into my consciousness.

Crawling towards Wholeness

I am in a pig pen and broken. It is not a pretty sight to be in the pigpen of sin: Filth. Smelly. Rottenness that sticks to your skin, mats your hair, and fills your soul. It's hard, oh so hard, to get clean. You can't even track your path to this pit of slime.

It wasn't always like this! One minute, life was a party. Then, in a blink, there was brokenness.

I shy away for lack of hope, sometimes I slink away in hurt or disillusionment, and sometimes I turn aside in willful disobedience. Something, though, keeps drawing me back to God. What? I ask myself. I dangle on a pendulum that swings from God's mercy to His wrath, back to forgiveness, and ends---where? Some never find wholeness.

I want to come home! There's only one clear view from the pigpen if only I would look up. I look up to the One Who can rescue me, and I listen to Him. God is calling.

What gives me hope, though, is that Jesus worked with whatever grain of faith a person might muster. He did after all, honor the faith of everyone who asked, from the bold centurion to doubting Thomas to the distraught father who cried, "I do believe; help me overcome my unbelief!"

In his autobiography, "A Long Walk to Freedom," Nelson Mandela recalls the scene when he first laid eyes on his granddaughter. At that time, he was working in hard labor on Robben Island in almost unbearable conditions, cutting lime in a quarry under a sun so bright that it nearly blinded him. Only one thing kept the prisoners from despair, he writes: they sang together as they worked. The songs reminded them of family, home and tribe and the world outside they might otherwise forget.

During the fourteenth year of his imprisonment, Mandela gained permission for a visit from his daughter (he was generally forbidden visitors).She ran across the room and embraced him. Mandela had not held his daughter since she was a young girl, and it was both poignant and dizzying to hug this fully grown woman, his child. Then she handed over her own newborn baby, Nelson's granddaughter, into his callused, leathery hands. "To hold a newborn baby, so vulnerable and soft in my rough hands, hands that for too long had held only picks and shovels, was a profound joy. I don't think a man was ever happier to hold a baby than I was that day."

Mandela's tribal culture had a tradition of letting the grandfather choose a new baby's name, and Nelson toyed with various names as he held that tiny, helpless baby. He settled on Zaziwe, which means Hope. "The name had special meaning for me, for during all my years in prison, hope never left me---and now it never would. I was convinced that this child would be a part of a new generation of South Africans for whom apartheid would be a distant memory---that was my dream."

Teilhard de Chardin expands on O' Connor's analogy of God as the artist:

"Like an artist who is able to make use of a fault or an impurity in the stone he is sculpting or the bronze he is casting, so as to produce more exquisite lines or a more beautiful tone, God, without sparing us the partial deaths, nor the final death, which form an essential part of our lives, transfigures them by integrating them in a better plan----provided we lovingly trust in Him. Not only our unavoidable ills but our faults, even our most deliberate ones, can be embraced in that transformation, provided always we repent of them.

Not everything is immediately good to those who seek God; but everything is capable of becoming good."

The *Hapag* was a healing journey towards wholeness. It is God's gift to me. Painting it was actually narrating facts of my life. It took me a jolt of tragedy and illness to create an existential crisis of faith. At such a moment, I wanted immediate clarity. "Lord, heal my woundedness and brokenness and make me whole again." It's only now that I realize that the day I got sick was actually the day I started living.

Let me end with the words of my favorite author Henri Nouwen:

"Our life is a short time in expectation, a time in which sadness and joy kiss each other at every moment. There is a quality of sadness that pervades all the moments of our life. It seems that there is no such thing as a clear-cut pure joy, but that even in the happiest moments of our existence, we sense a tinge of sadness. In every satisfaction, there is an awareness of limitations. In every success, there is a fear of jealousy. Behind every smile, there is a tear. In every embrace, there is loneliness. In every friendship, distance. And in all forms of light, there is the knowledge of surrounding darkness…But this intimate experience in which every bit of life is touched by a bit of death can point us beyond the limits of our existence. It can do so by making us look forward in expectation to the day when our hearts will be filled with perfect joy, a joy that no one shall take away from us."

At present, I am still crawling and struggling to get myself out of the dark and towards the light. Now, I am certain though that the light is not one which glitters momentarily and fades out instantly. I am aware that this light is getting brighter and brighter by the day.

a light which can never be extinguished by the strongest winds that destroy the sturdy trees and howl during the night. This light stays for all eternity and keep us aflame as the Spirit of God fuels us and breathes in us.

THEY HAVE JESUS

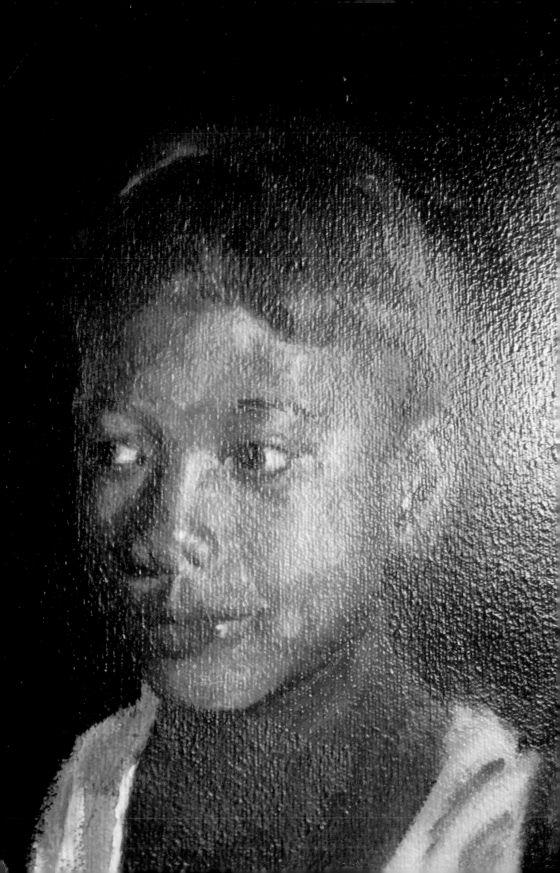

THEY HAVE JESUS

CHAPTER 8

Fragrance of the Dumpsite

"*'ano kinakain 'yong Pagpag? Masarap ba 'yon?*" [How do you eat Pagpag? Does it taste good?] I asked Michael, a thirteen-year-old boy scavenger in Payatas. He was my child model in a tattered shirt holding a paper plate with noodles while standing second from the right.

"*Papakuluan muna 'yon, tapos pipirito mo. Kung ayaw mo iprito, adobo. Lahat lahat hamburger, karne, etc.-paghahaluhaluin.*" [You boil it, then fry it. If you don't want to fry it, you cook it with vinegar and soy sauce. Everything-hamburger, meat, etc.all mixed together.] *Pagpag* refers to these blends that are derived from other rotten food which is sometimes taken from the same mound where dead cats, rats, dogs, and at times human cadavers with entangled parts are mixed.

"Ano ang lasa nu'n?" [How does that taste?]

"Maasim. Medyo panis na rin eh. Pero ok pa rin at least laman tiyan pa rin. Sa gabi wala na. Hindi na inaabot ng gabi. Special na 'yon eh." (It is sour coz' it's a bit spoiled already. But it's still okay, at least it fills the stomach. In the evening, we have no more food. It won't last until evening. That's already a special food.)

He was like a young chef of the garbage cuisine explaining a recipe which tasted like hell. I almost puked upon hearing the ingredients and concoctions of the most nauseating and disgusting dish preparation I have ever heard. It was gross.

Filth and Muck

While the rich children swim at the pool clubhouse in the posh villages of the Metropolis, Michael, one of the 40,000 scavenger kids, is seen digging into and eking out of a mountain of muck. He was also swimming....with a metal hook which looked like a sickle on his right hand which he calls.... *"kalahig"* and which he describes as *"parang karit na hindi naman baluktot."* [Like a straightened sickle.]It was a real symbol of death. Wearing a pair of thin dilapidated slippers, he does this awful activity of rummaging garbage to earn a living and to contribute for the food budget of their household. Unbelievable stench! I see young boys cover their faces with their T-shirts, guerilla style. Michael is just one of the many dozens of children, some

136

as young as two years old, who regularly go to the dump. But there is no disguising the fact that this is a garbage dump and that his work is filthy and degrading. The scavengers are the great levelers of society, recycling the remains of the city, perhaps to see it return as garbage.

Upon entering that vast dumpsite, a mayor's permission had to be first secured. It was a tightly guarded place by a security group called P.O.G.. It was so organized that those who scavenge wear IDs for government control and regulated local policy. The process starts with the garbage trucks, looking like a sort of serial intestinal tract, which arrive minutes apart, more than 400 a day, bringing 1,800 tons of garbage to the Payatas dump in 16-hour spans.Computers log them in as they arrive, but as in so many areas of life, those amazing machines cannot match the natural gifts of man. *"Alam namin kung s'an galing 'yong trak sa amoy pa lang,"* [We know where the trucks come from by the smell] said Michael. *"Magaling kaming suminghot."* (It's an inhalant skill), so to say. The stench was so fetid that it penetrates your clothes and skin. I remember now and I appreciate the fragrance of a durian fruit which never made it to our fruit basket. Four hot showers couldn't remove such a terrible smell which got to be so strong that I felt like throwing up.

With the other scavengers, he joins the hungry flies that swarm over the spilled guts of the city, in constant motion — bending, reaching, turning, tossing, lifting, digging, heaving — as the hot sun climbs into the sky and begins to sink again.

When it rains, the putrid flavors of the muck can send even lifelong professionals staggering down the sopping mountainside, their hands over their faces, the sludge slopping in over the tops of their rubber boots. In the dry months, trucks painted with the bright slogan "Service at its best" stir up a fine, foul dust, choking the lungs with an aerosol of waste. Dizzy and coughing, the scavengers dance with the wind, turning like weather vanes to keep the noxious powder at their backs.

"Nakita mo na ba 'yong sarili mo sa painting ko, Michael?"
[Did you see yourself in my painting Michael?] I asked the boy soaked in sweat with mud.

"Hindi pa. Ewan ko. Wala akong pakialam du'n." [Not yet. I don't know. I don't give a damn.]

Michael is a boy who considers himself part of the garbage. He considers his "being" made of garbage and steel. He was a real toughie. He was hardened by the cruelty of life's dirt. He was considered a "bad boy" in the dumps. He answered my questions in a seemingly impolite manner. But I understood...for he had every reason to be bitter.

"Paki kuwento mo nga ang buhay mo sa pananambakan."
[Please relate your story in the dump site.]

"Maraming ring nakukuha d'yan! Nangangalahig ako ng mga sibak-sibak. 'Yong mga plastic." [There are many things that can be retrieved from there. I collect big pieces. Plastic stuff.]

"Ba't sibak?" [Why sibak?]

"Binibili din 'yon. 'Yon ang tawag nila eh." [They buy those

138

too. That's how they call them.]

He was a rough boy I could sense. He was narrating how he was sometimes mobbed by a group of young bandits.

"Sinumpak nga ako buti nakailag ako. Pinalo ko kasi ng bato 'yon eh." [They hit me with a popgun, good thing I was able to dodge. I hit them with a rock.]

"Ba't mo pinalo?" [Why did you hit them?] I wondered.

"Tangna nangangalahig ako tangna pinagtripan ako eh." [I was collecting then they picked on me.]

"Ilan sila?" [How many were they?]

"Dalawa sila ng kuya n'ya?" [They were two: his older brother and he.]

" 'Pag nakita nila ako sa lugar nila delikado." [It's too dangerous once they see me in their territory.]

He started as a scavenger when he was seven years old. He said he was forced to work in order for his family to survive, mainly to be able to buy food. *"Araw-araw ako rito. Wala akong pakialam sa amoy. Tae nga kaya ko kainin eh. Importante sa akin gatas para sa utol kong bunso."* [I'm here every day. I don't care about the smell. I can even eat human waste. What's important is milk for my youngest sibling.] He skipped the childhood part of boy's growth, which was an unknown stage for him, and was forced by circumstances to grow old fast and to labor in the trash area.

"Bumibili ako ng bigas pangkain namin. Ang nanay ko wala d'yan. Nasa Sta Mesa. Wala na 'kong tatay. Lolo ko ang nag-aalaga sa amin. Nagpapakain s'ya ng baboy." [I buy rice for us to eat. My mother is not here. She's in Sta. Mesa. I don't have a father anymore. Our grandfather is the one taking care of us. He feeds pigs.] At the end of the day, he walks down the mountainside to his little home, a mile away, where his jobless grandfather and siblings are waiting.

Short of a topic to sustain the conversation, I tried a stupid one, *"May TV ba kayo sa bahay?"* [Do you have a TV in the house?]

"May TV kami. 'Tang inang 'yon sira naman. Nagloloko." [We have a TV. It's out of order again.]

"Tatlong kapatid ko nasa mama ko. Ako lang iniwan dito. Dito na ako lumaki. Mahirap buhay namin. Sa Montalban nasagasaan 'yong paa ko du'n ng trak. 'Yong kasama ko daming magkakapatid, sina Nano at Kadyo. Nangangalahig sila. Mga gago 'yon. 'Pag wala silang kinita hindi nila ibibigay sa magulang nila eh." [My three siblings are with my mother. I grew up here. Our life is difficult. In Montalban, my

foot was run-over by a truck. My companions have many siblings: Nano and Kadyo. They collect stuff. The fools! They don't give anything to their parents when they don't earn anything.)

"E wala namang kinita eh.? Ano ang ibibigay nila.?" [But they didn't earn anything. What will they give?] I was startled with his logic.

"Ewan ko sa kanila du'n." [I don't know.]

"Ikaw lahat binibigay mo?" [Do you give everything?]

"Oo." [Yes.]

"Magkano ang kinikita mo?" [How much do you earn?]

"P120"

"Malaki rin pala 'no?" [That's a big amount.]

"Paano kumikita ng pera du'n?" [How do you earn from there?] I questioned with a calculator in my left palm.

The bounty of the trucks is shifted and sorted by the scavengers, who pass it on to scrap shops specializing in copper wire, old newspapers, aluminum cans, plastic, cardboard, bits of machinery, box springs, raffle tickets, tires, broken toys — virtually all the infinite components of civilized life.

"'Yong sibak. Kung tawagin tulad ng plastic, bote, dyaryo, karton, bakal...sa junk shop dadalhin. Binebenta namin kay Joel Bulan." [The big pieces. That's how they are called; like plastic, bottles, newspapers, cartons, steel...they are brought to the junk shop. We sell them to Joel Bulan.]

"Trak ng basura ng Quezon City lang. Walang guwantes karami-han ang mga bata. 'Yong iba may bota, pero ako tsinelas lang." [They are brought to the truck of Quezon City. Many of the kids don't have gloves. Others have boots but I only wear slippers.]

"P'ano n'yo binubuhat 'yon?" [How do you carry them?]

"Sinusuong namin sa ulo. Hindi sa kariton. 'Yong ibang mga bata ang kita lang nila beinte hanggang singkwenta. Ako lang ang malaki. Iba-iba ang pinanggalingan. Sorsogon, Masbate, Bisaya, Gu-bat Sorsogon, Mindanao. Hanggang elementary ang pinakamataas na pinag-aralan dito. Grabe nu'ng natabunan 'yong tambakan, nu'ng nagka landslide. *Grabe 'yon! Binawalan na kaming mga bata na umakyat. Gipit sa pera ang mga bata rito."* [We place them on our heads. Not in the pushcart. The otherkids earn only P20-50. I'm the only one who earns a lot. People here come from various places. Sorsogon, Masbate, Visayas, Gubat Sorsogon, Minadanao. The highest educational attainment here is elementary. It was bad when the dump site was covered during a landslide. That was bad! We kids were prohibited from going up. Kids here lack money. Since then, the mountain has been graded to a gentler slope and the squatters have been moved outside a bright yellow security fence. Signs read, "No ID, no entry" and "Children under 14 not allowed."]

"Ano pa ang ibang trabaho mo?" [What are your other jobs?]

Smelling Danger

The group of Michael, however, also specializes in rotten food, mostly from restaurants and hotels, which they sell to a broker as feed for pigs. They also keep an eye out for plastic packing strips, which they bring home, clean and weave into baskets for sale. *"Hindi lang mga lata-lata, bote garapa, karton, at assorted ang kinokolekta namin"* [I don't only collect tin cans, bottles, cardboard, the usual stuff], Michael said. *"Maganda at madaling ibenta 'yong mga scrap"* [The scraps are better and easier to sell.]

"Pagkatapos mangalahig, manganganing baboy ako. Pinagbawalan na kami umakyat sa pinakatuktok. Delikado kasi. Du'n na lang kami sa hindi mataas na mga bundok." [After collecting, I put together the left-over food. We were prohibited from going up to the peak. It's because it's dangerous there. We just go to the places that are not very high.]

"Kaya hindi ako nakaakyat nang maayos kanina napaltok ako ng kalahig eh." [I was hit by a sickle on the head that's why I wasn't able to go far.]

"Napaltok ako. Namaga agad 'yong kamay ko. Tangna!." [My hand swelled immediately. Fuckin' shit.]

"Delikado pala mapaltok?" [It's dangerous to get hit?]

"'Yong kasama kong isa napaltok sa batok. Patay.

Pinagtripan s'ya sa may Suro. Tapos mapili ng may ari ng dumping, susuriin na. Tapos si Tuktok sumusunod sa bulldozer. Pinaltok sya sa batok. Kinabukasan patay. Baon 'yong kalahig sa bumbunan n'ya eh." (My companion was hit in the nape. He died. He was picked on near Suro. After the owner of the dumpsite gathers what he wants, he would sort out the spoils. Tuktok was following the bulldozer. He was hit on the head. The next day, he died. The sickle went deep into his head.)

"Ano ang nangyari du'n sa nakapatay?" [What happened to the one who killed him?)]

"Pinaghahanap na ng baranggay." [The barangay folk are looking for him.]

"Ano ang gusto mo paglumaki ka?" [What do you want to be when you grow up?] I asked him with hope that he would be lightened up and momentarily imagine a distant future with brighter hope ahead.

"Tangna hindi ko na iniisip 'yon." [Mother fucker. I don't think about that anymore.] I was shocked with such an answer.

"Nagdadasal ka ba?" [Do you pray?] I inquired in panic.

"Hindi ko na maisip 'yong mga 'yon," [I don't get to think about those anymore.] He answered in a disgusted manner.

"Nasubukan ko na rin mag 'rugby'," [I've tried sniffing rugby.] He added.

"Bakit ka nag'rurugby?" [Why do you sniff rugby?]

"Wala akong magawa eh!" [I have nothing else to do.]

"Masarap ba?" [Is it good?]

"Hmmm… oo. Nawawala ka na sa….ano….wala ka nang maisip? Basta trip trip trip ka na lang. Hindi na ako makapag-isip. Hindi na. Tang ina 'pag ako nagtitrip…babasagin ko ulo ng kasama ko. Papaluin ko nga sana 'yong kasama ko eh. Nabad trip ako eh pinagti- tripan ako eh. May hawak din s'yang bote. Paluin ko rin s'ya ngayon." [Hmmm…Yes. You lose your…you don't get to think of anything. You're just floating. I can't think anymore. Nope. When I'm high, I can break the head of my companion. I was about to hit my compan- ion. I was very much annoyed because he picked on me. He was also holding a bottle. I'll hit him now.]

I wanted to run away after hearing his statement to seek for cover. Street children are a common sight in Manila. You often see them on sidewalks, sniffing "rugby" and smoking crack to get high. But this one is of different stock. He braves all challenges and fears no death.

Being Humbled

When I invited him for a snack at Mcdonald's that same afternoon, he had no reaction of excitement whatsoever. He was just wearing a face of indifference. Like a savage with fierce eyes, he remained hostile. I realized that when you treat these children to any form of comfort like food or drink, and even when you serve them and accord them in a most gentle way, they just stare at you. They just look at you with suspicion and mistrust because they do not have any idea of what kindness is all about. Benevolence is foreign to them. Their world is crowded with the web of filth and dirt and skepticism that no intentions are considered well enough, considering that they live in an extremely harsh condition of life. Everything and everyone is garbage. I was struck by how Michael recounted to me in a very sarcastic way the *"bangkang papel"* (paper boat) of the State of the Nation's Address three years ago.

I suddenly remember the world where I live in. I have enjoyed a fairly good reputation in the industry were I belong. People believe every word I say and they regard my untainted name. They honor my work ethics and they respect each transaction we enter into. My suppliers consider my check as good check. Trust and confidence is the name of my game and gentlemen's agreement is more bankable than any written contract. I earned this in years of hard work and honest relations. But now, my humility is tested immensely.

It was quite depressing to be with Michael. I grumbled within. This perhaps was the reason why there are no sustainable livelihood programs for the poor in their place, I resented within. I felt that it was a challenge being good to this kind of boy. What do I get out of my gesture of affection? What benefit do I gain with my generous deed? I might not have the best answers. No, not in this lifetime probably. In this fashion, I share the insecurities of the poor when they are not accorded the proper credence, or when others prejudge them and second guess intentions and all. Was this not the experience of Christ Himself too?

I am convinced that what matters most is not how many people give importance and look highly at me or if they raise me on a pedestal. It is whether I have loved or not. In the end I will not be asked how much I have earned or how many people I have touched, but with how much love I have served the Lord. I take solace in the words of Mother Teresa of Calcutta in her Nobel Prize Acceptance Speech in 1979:

> "It is not enough for us to say: I love God, but I do not love my neighbor. St. John says you are a liar if you say you love God and you don't love your neighbor. How can you love God whom you do not see, if you do not love your neighbor whom you see, whom you touch, with whom you live. And so this is very important for us to realize that love, to be true, has to hurt. It hurts Jesus to love us, it hurts him. And to make sure we remember his great love he made himself the bread of life to satisfy our hunger for his love. Our hunger for God, because we have been created for that love. We have been created in his image. We have been created to love and be loved, and then he has become man to make it possible for us to love as he loved us. He makes himself the hungry one--the naked one--the homeless one--the sick one--the one in prison--the lonely one--the unwanted one--and he says: You did it to me. Hungry for our love, and this is the hunger of our poor people. This is the hunger that you and I must find; it may be in our own home."
> -Teresa of Calcutta

The crowning glory of Jesus' ministry was not His feeding the 5,000 when people were so elated that they wanted Him to be king, nor His triumphant entry to Jerusalem, but His crucifixion with only John and Mary to witness it at His feet and His resurrection with no one even to directly witness it.

Jesus promised us rest when He said "Come to me all you who labor and are burdened..." But that rest is premised on our ability and willingness to share Christ's yoke, and our openness to learn from Him meekness and humility. No yoke-sharing, no learning. Such learning, that blooms into meekness and humility, is possible for the Christian disciple, "if only the Spirit of God dwells in us" not the spirit of mistrust, discouragement, hopelessness, and pride.

My experience with Michael was not gratifying at first glance. Filth and muck. It was quite difficult because I had to submerge myself into the deepest realm of my sincerity in doing good. He has truly helped me mature in this regard. I realized that I did not feed Him. He actually fed me because there was hunger in me.

I wanted to share this poem which a young man composed. He was engrossed in it that he entered the priesthood.

THIS IS MY CROSS
(The Parable of the Poor Christ)

As the Poor becomes poorer
the nails are getting deeper.
As they cry out and perish, the thorns begin to pierce.
The blood of Christ is shed
When people scavenge for bread
The cross becomes heavy, when they're treated unjustly.

When we succumb to indifference,
To the needy across our fence,
Our Lord becomes weary
and dragged once more to Calvary.
Christ calls us once again
that heaven we may gain.
To follow him
we must dare
To carry the cross
and SHARE.

THEY HAVE JESUS

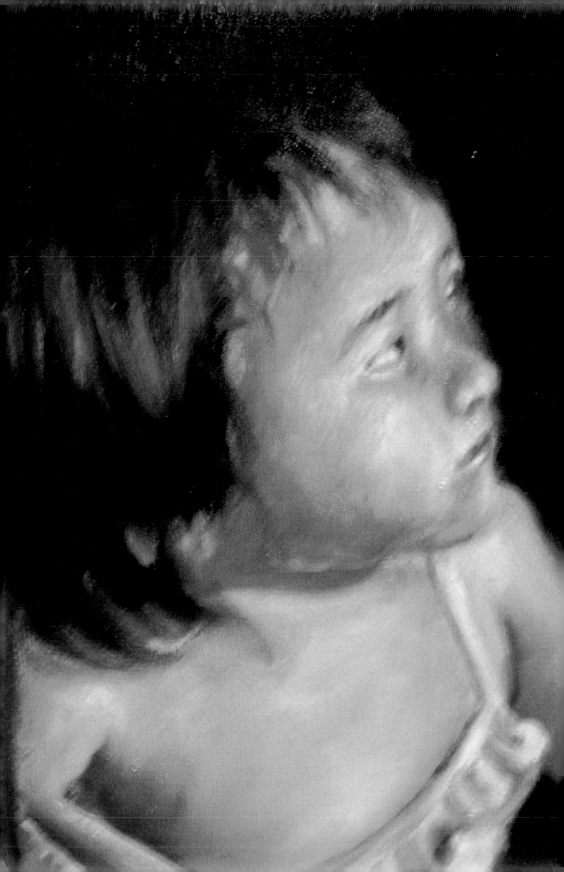

THEY HAVE JESUS

CHAPTER 9

The Doll of Tinay

"To see a world in a grain of sand,
And a heaven in a wild flower,
Hold infinity in the palm of your hand,
And eternity in an hour..."
(William Blake, Auguries of Innocence)

lank stares. Pale face. Wounded spirit. Not a single word can be heard from her tiny dry lips, not because she was shy. She just nibbled her thumb and caressed her dusty worn-out gray doll with the shattered cotton and nylon

fiber coming out of the cloth, the dolly toy lay lifeless with mangled fabric hands as if recently raped by a barbaric sexual moron. Both of them lived in a world of their own. An unwanted mark that has come to identify her. How can this stigma be removed so that people see her for the beautiful child she is and not simply as the survivor of a heinous experience? Sometimes, I realize how God sends thunder to stir us.

I am writing this chapter with trembling hands. I feel reluctant to narrate a very delicate story. Sometimes it's difficult to put the pain you feel into words. When someone's hurt, you can see the capacity for language being destroyed.

> "English, which can express the thoughts of Hamlet and
> the tragedy of Lear, has no words for the shiver and the
> headache...the merest schoolgirl, when she falls in love, has
> Shakespeare or Keats to speak her mind for her; but let a
> sufferer try to describe a pain in his head to a doctor and
> language at once run dry."

> Virginia Wolf

Trauma of Tiny Tinay

Christina is her name, but her neighbors call this tiny angel Tinay. She has withdrawn herself from people and she has lost her interest in playing. She always prefers to be alone and she trembles when she sees an older man. She lived in a place called Tumana (Not the real name); a place where she could be blemished for the rest of her life. Her mother works abroad as a contractual domestic helper

154

while her philandering father is a heavy user of drugs. She is the youngest of two daughters but the eldest has a family of her own to tend to. Her aunt, who has six children, would visit her in the gutter house from time to time.

"Ang nanay niya nasa ibang bansa. Tapos po ang tatay babaero na adik pa. Nakakulong. Lagi po s'yang napapabayaan tapos ang kapatid po nya na panganay may asawa na po ngayon, hindi na po s'ya maasikaso dahil may anak na po. 18 'yong edad nu'ng ate n'ya. Napilitan 'yong ate n'ya na mag-asawa dahil sa tatay nila. Kilala ko po ang ugali ni Emil. Sobra po sa droga 'yan eh. Kaya po laging malungkot at malayo ang tingin n'yang bata na 'yan eh." [Her mother is abroad. Then the father is a playboy and an addict. She is always neglected. Her eldest sibling who is married can no longer take care of her because she already has a child of her own. Her sister is 18 years old. She was forced to get married because of their father. I know Emil's character. He's into so much drug abuse. That's why Tinay is always sad and she has this 'far-away' look.]

"Kaya pala sobrang tahimik si Tinay? Ba't di nagsasalita? Malung-kutin." [So that's why Tinay is so quiet. Why doesn't she speak? She's always sad.]

"Umiiyak nga po 'yan palagi. Meron pong nangyari sa kanyang masama...Nakakaawa s'ya. Muntik nga po magkahemoreyds yan. Nasa malayo po kasi 'yong nanay n'ya eh." [She cries all the time. Something bad happened to her… She's so pitiful. She almost had a hemorrhage. Her mother is far away.]

"Ilang taon na si Tinay?" [How old is Tinay?] I asked her aunt.

"Limang taon lang po 'yan. Kahapon birthday po n'ya." [She's only 5 years old. It was her birthday yesterday.]

"Nasa'n na 'yong tatay niya?" [Where is her father?]

"Sa bilangguan po. Kahit durugin po ang buto at gawing betsin, kulang pa." [In prison. Even if his bones were crushed and made into vetsin, that would not be enough.]

"Pakita natin 'yong picture n'ya sa painting ko..." [Let's show her picture in my painting.]

Tinay was the only person looking at Jesus in the *Hapag* Painting. She was just side glancing though, as if asking herself, "Who is this male person...again? Is this goodness for real?" She was the youngest character, next to the stray kitten. I could not remember seeing her eat anything during that scene. Not that she was full, but perhaps she was afraid to be with people. She was like a toy whose battery has lost power.

"Mahal ba talaga tayo ng Diyos? Bakit may mga sobrang demonyo na sumisira sa kinabukasan ng tao at mga bata?" [Does God really love us? Why are there evil persons who destroy the future of people and of children?]

Her aunt asked this question while staring sharply at the painting poster, as if laser fire was coming out of her eyes and gradually burning my painting to ashes. This was a question which definitely rose up from a suffering and broken heart. I was startled. I was hard pressed to give a quick and convincing answer. I wanted to tell her concerned aunt, sincere in her pain, and sincere in her frustrations, that I, too, shared her pain; that I, too, grappled with the same questions ; that I, too, wanted quick, not round-about answers that all led to the depths of mystery, the twisted and convoluted pathways of an answer to a question that had bothered, and still bothers the best and the brightest of minds down through human history. In the novel *"El Filibusterismo,"* this was Simoun's million dollar question to Padre Florentino. This has been a recurrent question and complaint against a God of freedom, a God who sometimes is perceived like Christ "sleeping on a cushion" somewhere at the back of the boat being tossed about by murderous waves. Where is God when we need Him most? Where is God when a father raped his daughter one sunny and bright morning? When will we be freed from darkness?

Tinay is as damaged as her doll. I really doubt whether she can get proper education in her present condition. Her future is bleak. I immediately realized that in taking on this endeavor and in the hope of healing this bruised little girl, I was also taking on the responsibility to answer her when she finally opened her mouth and asked the question - WHY? All I could do was give her back a blank stare perhaps. I couldn't help but think of my four kids, especially my four-year-old girl Clarisse who is almost the same age as the reference model. Sometimes, before going to bed, they would all scamper off to their pillows when I turn off the lights. Though not necessarily psychologically sound, I announce that the monster is coming, in my desire to let them remain in their places. There were moments when they would request for a horror story or two or ask me to play the DVD of "The Exorcist" which I keep in a secret compartment. It is sometimes fun and creepy to embrace each other under our big blanket which we convert into a tent or a dome at times.

In the life of Tinay, the MONSTERS are real. It is not fiction or the rubber masks of Frankenstein we slip our heads into. It is reality for her and it keeps on coming back not only at night but even in her nightmares which happen during the day. She doesn't need any disc movie to watch the frightening scenes. These episodes keep on playing back...frame-by-frame like a jog shuttle every time she casts those blank stares.

The heinous crime of child rape shocks us as none other. Parents' substance abuse problems affect the life of the children, with catastrophic consequences. When we asked the children for the reasons behind their sadness, the most common were problems within the family, especially the parents' abuse of alcohol. Poverty is indeed very debilitating to men who are reduced to living like animals. They become predators when they are dehumanized and stripped of their natural male nobility. Men, by their very nature, are meant to be datus, pandays, hunters, and protectors of their families, at least in our culture. As Filipinos, men are expected by society to be the providers. Caught in the cycle of poverty and being unable to deliver as they are expected to, Pinoy males lose all motivation to be productive members of society and instead turn towards vices of drinking, gambling, mendicancy and some even turn to a life of violence to regain their primacy over society.

Storms of Life

I can't imagine a small and helpless creature like Tinay braving a storm. She has no idea about how to defend herself. Where can she draw her strength? She can easily be blown by the slightest wind and rain. She has no concept of strength. She can be thrown anytime by the gigantic wave. Unlike the adults, she is so weak. Yes, there are storms that challenge us, but we are equipped with so much courage because of age and experience to parry the blows of any hurricane. Because we are adults, we were given the capacity to face and stand strong amidst the storms that come our way, storms that hit us and storms that we have caused others too. It was a storm like that on the Sea of Galilee that Mark described in the Gospel. Surrounded by mountains on three sides and measuring only four miles across, the Sea of Galilee was a prime target for the most ferocious onslaughts of nature. Mark's record of this storm certainly emphasized God's power over nature.

No one can escape such storms. Our goodness or our faith cannot insulate us from the common experiences of life. Tragic events come into our lives regardless of who we are. And they sometimes strike so suddenly. We can only survive the storms of life if we have a strong sense of who is with us in the midst of the storm. The disciples in their terror forgot that. Christ was with them and guiding them safely to the other side. To what abysmal depths their faith sank when they awoke Him with the words, "Do you not care that we perish?" What horrific words were those? How could they question His concern in light of all that they had witnessed? He had healed the sick, fed the hungry, given solace to those in grief. Their insensitivity must have cut Him to the core. They lost their trust momentarily. His strong words brought them back to faith in his power to see us through. Later on they would hear His words, "Go into the world… and lo, I am with you to the end of the age." With their renewed faith they went out and told the story that has changed the world.

C.S. Lewis writes, "God whispers to us in our pleasures, speaks in our conscience, but shouts in our pains. It is His megaphone to rouse a deaf world." Maybe you've been deaf to God lately. Maybe you're an unbeliever who's been deaf to God your entire life. These kinds of situations should wake you up and lead you to think, "Am I prepared to face the greater judgment that's coming?"

In the end, abstract answers really don't matter. Highfalutin philosophical and theological tenets won't clinch it. I can never forget the summer camps in Baguio when I was growing up. We would wake up as early as 2 am and trek as a group up to Sto. Tomas peak. With backpacks and canteens around our waist, we young hikers would grab a branch which we could use as a staff or just to shovel away some horse's shit. As I approached the ledge, I saw a huge tree devastated by a freak ball of lightning. I even saw a lifeless goat amidst the old tree blown by the explosive force. I think of that scene sometimes when I scramble down a trail above timber line, glancing every few seconds at an angry thunderhead closing in. An old climber once observed that mountains are neither fair nor unfair, they just simply sit there. Perhaps, but when I am standing on an exposed ledge, enveloped in immensity, vulnerable to hail, blizzards, lightning, and other dangers, I feel very small and very fragile. Any hubris I picked up living a very comfortable life melts away. Nature reminds me how dependent and frail I am, how mortal.

> *There's no storm strong enough to tear you away from your source of strength. No pain can hide the Savior from you.*
> *No disappointment can derail your journey to the Father.*
> *It's a matter of will ~ that continual leap of faith you make when your spirit is bruised.*

Can Hope Heal?

My friends kept affirming me no end that without my knowledge of it, many people had been healed and are being healed by my painting in so many ways. They say that many have become a little more charitable because they were touched by the emotionally charged and statement-filled concept expressed in the work. Some became compassionate not necessarily to poor kids but to poor people in general, including the elderly and those who labor and toil. Others may have been more generous not only to those who were in need but also to those who are poor in a different sense. It also spoke of the ills of our nation and the issue on social justice. Ripple effects of love filled those who have seen it. It gives me joy when they tell me that the message of HOPE had come across.

I have always asked myself, am I just a painter or do I also give hope in real life? Can I also give hope? Have I become a *"Hapag ng Pag-asa"* [Table of Hope] to others? This has been a challenge for me.

People's lives have been devastated by different storms that have attacked them. Is there even a spark of hope they can cling to when they see me? We were admonished by Jesus to see Him in the least of our brethren. Can each of them on the other hand see the face of God shining in us every time we encounter them and touch their lives? Or are they supposed to seek refuge because they see another storm in us that may imminently ruin their lives? Do my words strike others like lightning or do they liberate and inspire them towards freedom?

The painting invites us not necessarily with optimism, but with hope. I was trying to suggest that Christians are not, and ought never, to be bleary-eyed optimists alone. Whilst optimism can help us all face the destabilizing waves of challenges that rock the boat of our life and our faith, ultimately, it is not what we wish to see that would strengthen us, but what God wants us to see through the eyes of faith – and HOPE!

Are we "Hapag ng Pag-asa" to our fellowmen?

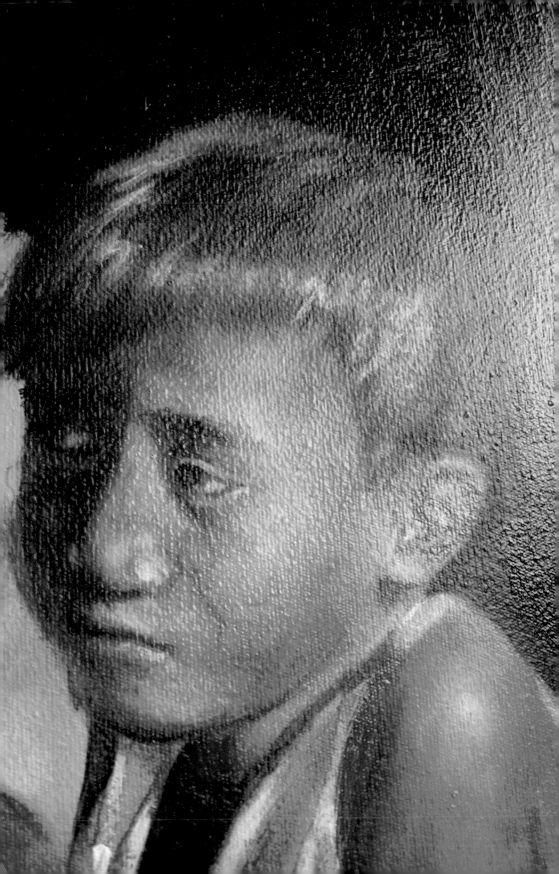

THEY HAVE JESUS

CHAPTER 10

Rumors of the Underworld

Nights without stars. Days without sunshine. You keep looking for a ray of hope to hold onto, but there is none. This is the life of those who live under the bridge. Most of the bridges in Metro Manila, if not all, have communities underneath. In their dark underworld, six meters below, they huddle against the pipes of the sewers, snatching fitful sleep, amid the stench, and scurrying rats resentful of this human invasion of their territory. At dawn, the children crawl out, covered in rat bites, fleas and sores. At daytime, they fan out into the market areas scavenging for food and stealing from passers-by.

Just outside the bustling Commonwealth Avenue, a sewer entrance serves as the home to a shifting population of 50 or 60 lost souls. They live precariously under the bridge where they cannot be seen. They sleep on the banks of our murky rivers and esteros, where most of us dare not go. Others descend into the sewers to seek shelter...They are the culvert and drainage squatters.

And this is where DODOY lives.

He is the coolest among all the little disciples. Coolest in the sense that he lives near the running waters. Dodoy is the boy in a faded blue sando at the far right of the Hapag painting. He is one of the apostles who was so difficult to find. Since last year, his family has transferred from one village under the bridge to another. With the kind help of Judith, my assistant, we were able to finally locate him in the third house where they were relocated.

Aside from the fast vehicles threading the vast highway, there was no space where we could park our car. The concrete cliff was so stiff and there was nothing to hold onto on that adobe brick-like wall as I descended into the underworld. With my cameras and tape recorder around my belt, my pants almost went down as I finally landed in the kingdom of more than thirty families living in that place "down under." As if I was in another world. My voice echoed as I asked around regarding where to find the boy, while holding the faded and almost shattered picture in my hand. "Oh, his name is Dodoy. He is in school right now," says the old woman in sarong clothes. She was courteous enough to direct us to the house where Dodoy lives. They call it "Koob-koob." It's as small as a pigpen, one meter high, just enough for them to survive horizontally for they would bump their heads standing up. Vivian, the mother, was there to welcome me.

"Good afternoon po, sir." [Good afternoon, sir.]

"Good afternoon. Nasa school daw po si Dodoy?" [Good afternoon. Dodoy is in school, I was told?]

"Opo, pero parating na 'yon maya-maya lang. Bakit po?" [Yes, but he'll be here in a little while. Why?]

"Ako po 'yong nag-imbita sa kanila last year para magshooting kasama si Kristo sa pagkain. Wala ba s'yang kinuwento sa inyo?" [I was the one who invited them for a 'shooting' (picture-taking) with Jesus while eating. Has he not told you anything?]

"Ah meron po. Parang nagpakain daw kayo ng sopas at nagbigay ng mga libro. Binabasa pa nga niya 'yon. Pero du'n pa 'yon sa dati naming tirahan." (Yes, he he did mention something like that. You fed

167

them with soup and gave them books. He still reads the books. But we lived in another place then.)

"Andito po sana ako para kumustahin sya. Medyo ang hirap lang po hanapin ng lugar n'yo. Buti may picture kami na naipakita sa mga dating tinirhan n'yo." (I'm here to find out how he is. It's just difficult to find your place. It's a good thing I was able to show a picture there in the place where you used to stay.)

"Marami po kasi kaming beses nademolish eh. Dito nga po mala-pit na naman eh pinatagal lang nang konti nu'ng kapitan sa Phase 5... pero pinapawasak na din daw po ni Bayani Fernando." (Our abode was demolished several times. Here, our place will be demolished soon; the captain of Phase 5 was able to extend a bit our stay but Bayani Fernando has given instructions to demolish it.)

I told her in jest that they were so lucky compared to other squatters because they have a very durable roof made of concrete, un-like the ordinary houses made of thin sheets of roof and at times rusty and with big holes where rain water can drip through. She laughed and said, *"Oo nga po eh. Kaya lang madalas naman kaming mauntog."* (Yes. It's just that we often bump our heads on the concrete ceiling.)

They built their houses underneath the walls of the bridge where there was really no room anymore for them to stand. Either they sit down or lie on the dirty cardboard scraps. When their hus-bands go out, they just roll from their improvised beds until they fall outside. I was listening to her but I could not look straight at her face because she was breastfeeding her youngest baby in front of me without inhibition.

"Pero buti may mga poste sa highway. Naiilawan din po kayo kahit papa'no" [But it's a good thing there are light posts along the highway. Your place gets lit up somehow.]

"Madilim din 'pag gabi. Kahit araw madilim kaya madalas dito kami nagpapasuso sa labas ng mga anak namin." [It's dark also at night. Even during daytime it's dark that's why we often breastfeed our children here outside.]

I looked down as she spoke. They don't have electricity at all. Some of them have TV sets from their old locations but they are useless now because they have no outlets to which they can plug their appliance. This was one of the reasons perhaps why there is population explosion under the bridge. Almost all the women curiously watching while I interviewed Vivian (the mother of Doy) were cuddling a baby in their arms. Almost all were breastfeeding too. I had no choice but really to look down, but as I grew tired I also talked raising my eyes to the sky. The tattooed men who were around were also watching closely where I directed my eyes.

"Buti naman po nakakapasok sa school si Dodoy." [It's a good thing Dodoy can go to school.]

"Ay opo. Talagang niraraos namin siya dahil 'yong ibang kapatid n'ya hindi nag-aaral. At masipag naman kasi 'yong bata." [Oh, yes, we really make it a point to spend for him to go to school because his siblings are not able to study. And Dodoy is truly hardworking.]

As I was speaking, Dodoy came down and jumped together with two buddies who came from a nearby public school. They were tired and their very old uniforms were soiled with the dirt of the highway where they riskily walked. He smiled and recognized me. He was amused while viewing the painting where he posed so naturally among kids he didn't know, after having a hearty meal with Jesus. He was a shy boy and a soft-spoken one at that. I told him how eager I was to meet him again.

"Marami ka rin bang kaibigan dito?" [Do you also have many friends here?]

"Opo si Robin. Kaya lang 'di ko na po makita. Napag-utusan pong magnakaw ng bakal. Pinadala nga po s'ya sa barangay eh. Tapos pinabalik s'ya sa bahay. May mga kasama rin sya. Lupeng ang pangalan at Miyao kapatid ni Jango." [Yes, there is. Robin. But I haven't seen him. He was ordered to steal some metal. He was sent to the barangay. Then he was sent back home. He also had companions. Their names are Lupeng and Miyao the siblings of Jango.]

"Di bale magkikita din kayo nu'n." [Don't worry. You'll see each other eventually.]

"Baka hindi na. Dedemolishin na 'yong bahay namin eh. Lilipat na kami." [Maybe not anymore. Our house will be demolished soon. We'll transfer soon.]

"Masaya ka ba na ininvite ka ni Jesus d'yan sa picture?" [Are you glad that Jesus invited you in the picture?]

"Kung narito si Jesus hindi kami madedemolish. Kaibigan s'ya eh." [If Jesus were here, our place will not be demolished. He's a friend.]

This 8-year-old boy goes to class but lacks the necessary books and notebooks to keep his education going. He is studious, according to his mother but does not have the needed materials.

I could see his father at a distance lying on their makeshift bed. He was snoring as he slept. His father has chronic ulcer and can hardly work. He sleeps all day because at night he is widely awake to guard his two elder sisters who are at risk of getting sexually molested by drunkards who loiter when everyone is asleep. He is a weakling, but he tries to protect his family from harm.

"Wala nga po trabaho 'yang mister ko. Paminsan-minsan na-kakapagbenta ng mineral water at kropek sa itaas. Kaya lang kailangan din po ng puhunan dahil naniningil agad 'yong kinukuhanan namin. Mabait naman po 'yan. Wala lang swerte talaga." (My husband does not have a job. Sometimes, he's able to sell mineral water and kro-peck up on the bridge. But he also needs capital because our supplier charges right away. My husband is good. He just doesn't have luck.)

"Sa'n kayo kumukuha ng panggastos?" (Where do you get money for your expenses?)

"Tulung-tulong po. Minsan naglalabada po ako. Pero pagnagkasu-nud-sunod ang problema, wala kaming magawa." (We help each other. Sometimes I do other peoples' laundry. But when problems come one after another, we can't do anything.)

Experience of Powerlessness

It is "water under the bridge" now, but she was narrating how a few months ago, they were in a deep crisis situation. Their baby was sick with high fever and was confined in a public hospital. She was shivering for many days and almost died of dehydration. Their hospital bill had reached as high as seven thousand and she didn't know where to go for help. She was crying profusely because back home there was a storm and the water was reaching waist-high and it almost swept away their only valued Koob-koob house away. She was so devastated and her world fell apart. Her husband recoiled in his bed crying and bearing the excruciating stomach pain that weakened him. They didn't have money for medicine or the cheapest pain reliever. Her other children didn't eat for two days. They just drank rain water from the drainage. Little Dodoy was the one gathering their things for safety under the heavy rain while holding his dog named "Tigre," which finally drowned. They were helpless and powerless.

I realized how extremely hard it is to be hopeless and powerless. You pick yourself up a little, dust yourself off and darn! Another crisis, another disappointment knocks you to the ground, and what do you do? When you're mired in the sticky swamp of hurts, how do you climb out? You're totally lost in the labyrinth of fear and helplessness. Everyman has his own experience of powerlessness. In those moments, we grope in the dark desperately seeking for whatever strength we can hold on to. In those shattering experiences, there is not a single iota of power left.

In the last scene of the award-winning Filipino film "*Maynila sa Kuko ng Liwanag* "(Manila in the Claws of Neon, 1975), you will see the protagonist being pursued and pinned down by a mob on a dead-end street. Yes, he was holding a dagger, but it appeared as a tiny needle before a mad and angry crowd which was ready to beat him and eventually kill him. The classic ending was that legendary extreme close up of Julio Madiaga's face— shocked and terrified. His widely opened mouth couldn't emit a single sound. A portrait of powerlessness.

Powerlessness. Away from the comfort zone. We become vulnerable. We not only experience being physically down but emotionally and psychologically as well. Even our morale dies and we're pulled down by our limitations. Restless, we can only do so much. This is the time when the grace of God can be so much at work. Because finally we say, "I surrender. I cannot do anything anymore. I failed. I'm helpless!" That's the time that Jesus' grace can work all the more. It seems we become overly self-sufficient when we are physically and emotionally strong. Whenever we are weak, we are at a loss as to where to gasp for air, for life.

"But He said to me, 'My grace is sufficient for you, for My power is made perfect in weakness'... For when I am weak, then I am strong."

(2 Corinthians 12:9-10)

Christ Sharing in the Powerlessness of Man

In the Hapag painting, highly noticeable was the sad face of Christ. Many have observed His sad demeanor. The mother of Dodoy asked, *"Ay, ba't ang lungkot ng mukha ni Jesus? Sana man lang pinasaya n'yo s'ya nang kaunti dahil pag-asa ang pinag-uusapan diyan eh. Parang talunan si Jesus ah. Di, mo man mabasahan sa mukha N'ya ang silay ng pag-asa."* [Why is Jesus' face sad? I wish you had made it look happy because the painting speaks of hope. Jesus looks defeated. You can't even catch a glimpse of hope from his face.] Jesus was staring blankly at the bread which He breaks in utter loneliness as if asking Himself, "After this simple meal, what next?..."

The poverty is so vast in this world that the Lord Himself felt weak. Yes, He was dining with these hungry children in the slums, but He seems defeated. It was as if He were saying, "How long will these kids live? How long will their bodies last?" And He shakes his head in utter surrender.

In this painting, He became one with us in experiencing power-lessness. He is united with us in weakness. The strong young Carpenter who surveys the ragged landscape of pain is here with us...broken. Isaiah wrote "When they suffered, he suffered also" (Isa. 63:9). On that dilapidated table made of scrap wood, Jesus must have suffered much. Though he is God, He felt helpless and He was hit by the sense of failure.

It is not right that He is the only one feeding others. It has to be the world doing it too. It has to be the people doing it also. His frustration here is his apparent inability to touch the hearts of others to do what He is doing for these children. Perhaps He is asking and challenging us.. "After I break this bread and share it with these children, is there tomorrow?"

This image reminds me about the words in the book of Revelation. "Here I am! I stand at the door and knock. If anyone hears My voice and opens the door, I will come in and eat with him, and he with Me." (Rev 3:20)

This is HAPAG isn't it? We welcome Him as our table companion. There is no activity among us Filipinos that better expresses the intimacy and the pleasure in each other that friends enjoy than to share a meal together. If we want somebody to know we esteem him, what do we do? We invite him to dinner. If we want somebody to know we would like to get better acquainted with him, we invite him to dine with us. Everybody understands. This is where friendship

begins and is concretized, in table fellowship. It has always been that way in our society. So, when Jesus says, "I will eat with him and he with Me," He is promising that He will be our companion, our intimate friend. Could there be any better companion, any better friend than He?

This image was also the inspiration of the Masterpiece of Holman Hunt, an English artist whose painting was entitled "The Light of the World." When he was ready to unveil it for the first time, he called his friends and family together to be the first to see it. It is a picture of Jesus Christ knocking at the door. In one hand He holds a lantern, and with the other He knocks at a wooden cottage door. The entrance is overgrown with vines, as though it has not been opened for a very, very long time. That painting was also inspired by a verse from the Book of Revelation. It was pretty quiet as each person stood there and drank in the deep feeling that painting conveys. Then people began to comment on what impressed them about it. But one critic raised a significant observation.

"It's a beautiful painting. There is one important detail however which you forgot to paint. There is no doorknob! How can that door be opened without the door handle?" The painter explained that it was intentionally done because that kind of door can only be opened from inside and not from the outside. It symbolizes the door of your heart. It can only be opened from within. Powerful as God is, He can easily open any door from the outside. He doesn't gatecrash. He just taps gently and knocks patiently. He allows us to open with our free will to show Him how we welcome Him into our hearts.

"Hapag ng Pag-asa" is an ironic painting because Jesus looks sad. There seems to be no ray of hope in that dinner gathering. Every face, including that of Christ, seems drowned in the darkness of gloom. In the same way, the doorknob to resolve the irony lies within.

It becomes a real "Hapag ng Pag-asa" depending on the people who look at it. The pag-asa would come with each one doing his share. It doesn't end with the picture. It continues with us. So Jesus is asking, "Having seen this seemingly defeated stance in the Hapag scene, what do you do NOW?" Can we welcome hope which is Christ Himself? It's an open-ended story. Can I tell Dodoy that I can be the ray of hope for him so I can at least make the face of Christ smile? Can I do this to prove that Christ's death was not worthless; that there was meaning in what He did in the offering of His life, because we are RESPONDING? It cannot be that He is always the One. We ought to give our share. We ought to open our door, let His graces come in and allow ourselves to be used to help others, especially the poor.

In the stage play *"God in the Dock"*, Jesus was put on trial and was cross-examined. They had to prove Him guilty for all the sufferings in this world. The prosecutor turned to Him and said,

"In the face of all these, what do You feel?"

Jesus in the hot seat said, "I feel a heavy pain in My heart."

"You can say those words in spite of the sufferings that You see everywhere?"

"Yes. If I were in their shoes, (referring to the complainants) I would also feel the same way."

To which the prosecutor said. "Then what are You doing? Given all the sufferings of this world, what are You doing???"

"I am talking to you, Anna." He called the prosecutor by name. He did not address her as attorney or your honor.

"What do you mean?" she asked.

"It's so easy to shift the burden or to pass the blame onto someone else. Let the government do it, let the Church do it. Let the priests do it, when in fact you too have a lot to do for the society."

Then the prosecutor said, "You must have forgotten. You're on trial here. Not me."

It is a thought-provoking scene, but one reason people choke on the idea of a loving God is that the world is this way. They ask, how can an all-powerful, all-loving God allow a world, which He supposedly loves, to get into such a mess? We fail to ask ourselves what we have done to worsen or either improve the situation. We fail to tell ourselves that we too must have our share, no matter how little, in releasing this world from bondage.

Two thousand years ago, Jesus amazed thousands of people in the multiplication of the loaves. It is unfair, we might reckon, that He does not do it now when billions are hungry. How can He bear the sight under the bridge where the children's big intestines eat their small intestines because there was scarce rice to digest in their tummy? How can He not perform this classic miracle we hope for and want to witness before our naked eyes?

No, our Lord does not do that alone in one flick of His holy fingers. There were the initial five loaves of bread and two fishes in the first place that were contributed. The multiplication of the loaves TODAY should happen with our participation. Imagine the face of Jesus while on table with the children. He raises His eyes to us and asks us, "Where are the five pieces of loaves that you can share, so that I can perform the long-awaited miracle of multiplication?" Perhaps He cannot find the five loaves and two fishes around that's why the Savior's face is rather long; that's why He looks defeated. Nary was there any offer of five loaves and two fishes. There is no door with a knob inside that opens. The Hapag ng Pag asa would only be a reality when people see this taking place; when people who care can make a difference in the lives of others.

The Bridge of Sighs

My brief experience with Dodoy's family reminds me of that bridge in Venice, Italy called "Ponte di Sospiri" (The Bridge of Sighs). It is made of white limestone material. This enclosed bridge has windows with stone bars. The name was invented in the 19th Century, when Lord Byron helped to popularize the belief that its name was inspired by the "sighs" of condemned prisoners as they were led through it to the executioner. The prisoners who passed through it on their way to the prison cells on the other side would most likely see their final view of beautiful Venice out the window before being taken down to their guillotine. It is seeing freedom for the last time. Their sigh would mean regret and anguish for such a beautiful life they have to leave because of a crime they have commited.

The bridge of Dodoy is my own version of the Bridge of Sighs. Before my very eyes, I saw the absence of what the world regards as beauty. Amid the stench, and scurrying rats, I sigh in disbelief because of what I witness before my eyes. I cannot imagine where my weary heart and restless soul have brought me. Before I left the place, I was surprised when they requested me to come back to gather them for Bible study. When I heard that, I sighed, "They also hunger for spiritual bread, but how can I share with them the love of God, when they experience hunger? How can they relate with a living Father in heaven when their own fathers do not show them love?"

I felt so powerless. It is easier for me to mount a canvas and paint their portraits than to share the Bible. It seems no one is listening as their pangs and wailings echo in that dark world under the bridge. When I look at the face of Dodoy, I see hope. I sigh not only because of its beauty but because of the wondrous and unlimited possibilities that may take place in this boy if only he can be supported and be given the chance to have a better life ahead. I sigh because I find myself in the prison of selfishness everytime I miss the chance to show God's love.

In the book of Isaiah 35:3 it says: "Strengthen the feeble hands, steady the knees that give way; say to those with fearful hearts, be strong, do not fear; your God will come, He will come with vengeance; with divine retribution. He will come to save you."

As I struggled to climb out of their hidden barangay, the women, in Bayanihan spirit, pushed my butt and my heavy body all the way up the bridge. I saw the glaring light; the hustle and bustle on the busy highway again. I saw the dusty earth from a different view. I felt uncomfortable with the comfortable world I live in. I looked down and said goodbye to Dodoy and he waved back at me...with hope renewed on his face.

"He gives strength to the weary and increases the power of the weak. Even youths grow tired and weary, and young men stumble and fall; but those who hope in the Lord will renew their strength. They will soar on wings like eagles; they will run and not grow weary, they will walk and not be faint." (Isaiah 40:29)

THEY HAVE JESUS

THEY HAVE JESUS

CHAPTER 11

The Scars of Joyce

Has anybody seen or heard a child giving birth to another child? I gulped as I learned that the straight-haired girl second from left (in the Hapag painting) was a mother already. A little young mother. Almost a year ago, Joyce delivered the baby in a government hospital. I wouldn't know this story had I not come back and looked for this small apostle of fourteen (her age when she posed for Hapag). I never knew that this could happen. She remained isolated and stayed with the baby all day long as if they were just sisters.

"Totoo ba 'yon Ate Mercy?" I asked the mother. [Is it true Ate Mercy?]

185

"Nanganak s'ya nu'ng kinse s'ya. Nu'ng una, 'kala namin may bukol o kaya tumor s'ya sa t'yan, pinaalbularyo pa namin. 'Kala namin nakulam. Di s'ya nagsasalita hanggang lumipat nga kami rito dahil nahiya na rin mga lola n'yan. Galit na galit. Apat na buwan na pala. Nagpatingin kami sa ospital. Ayun nga. Buntis. Ang liit liit pa nakakaawa. 'Kala namin mamamatay." [She gave birth when she was 15. At first we thought she had a lump or tumor in her stomach. We brought her to the quack doctor. We thought she was a victim of witchcraft. She was not speaking until we transferred to this place because her grandmothers were getting ashamed. They were so angry. She was already 4 months on the way. We had her checked in the hospital. We found out she was pregnant. She's still young, and how pitiful. We thought she would die.] She began speaking with inhibition and fear too ashamed of the fate her child had befallen.

"Noong una nga po, nahihiya kami lumabas dito dahil pinaguusapan nila lahat. Ang mga tao tsismisan tungkol sa kanya. Ang aga raw n'ya lumandi. Pero wala. Nasanay na rin kami." [At first, we were ashamed to go out of the house because people were talking about her. They were gossiping about her. They said she flirted very early. But we eventually got used to it.]

I couldn't believe what I heard. That meant to say that she had sexual intercourse (or was forced to do it) when she was just fourteen. I felt dizzy with such a puzzling yet painful story which was again stranger than fiction. It was not a movie flick. It was reality before my naked eyes. Perhaps the most discomforting truth, aside from early pregnancy and sex being an experience we associate with physical and psychological maturity, is the fact that it also implies the commission of an act now considered to be nothing less than child molestation.

"Sino po ang ama ng bata?" [Who is the father of the child?]

"Aling bata?... [Which child?] (verifying if I meant Joyce or her baby)
" 'Yong anak po ni Joyce..." I clarified smilingly. [The baby of Joyce…]

"Ah du'n pa sa Masbate 'yong hayop na 'yon. Ayaw magsalita n'yan

nu'ng una. Dahil takot. Pinadampot nga ng lolo 'yong gagong 'yon eh. Nakakulong nga ngayon 'yong demonyo na 'yon sa city jail eh. Nasabit sa droga." [Ah, that animal stays in Masbate. She didn't want to talk in the beginning because she was scared. Her grandfather asked the police to capture him. That devil is now imprisoned in the city jail. He was involved in drugs.]

She seemed to be quite uncomfortable to disclose the identity of the father and I respected her hesitancy on that regard. Near the blanket hammock, Joyce clutches her 9-month-old baby Temtem close to her chest and beams with pathetic pride.

" Eh, nasa'n naman po ang ama ni Joyce?" [Where is the father of Joyce?]

"Ang tatay po nito nasa Cavite. Bihirang bihira umuwi. Wala kasing makapalit sa pagluluto ng balat ng lumpia sa palengke ng Imus. Dating kontraktor ng NAWASA sa mga pipe line. Iniwan kaming lahat sa Masbate tapos 'yong mga pinsan po nu'n, nagnakaw ng mga tanso mga bakal ibinenta po sa junkshop kaya nahuli po sila kaya po natanggal po ang tatay nito sa trabaho tapos naging ...kumapit po sa patalim. Eto pong si Joyce bunso na po di na namin mapakain....nadagdagan pa." [Her father is in Cavite. He hardly comes home. He can't find a replacement in cooking the spring roll wrapper in the market of Imus. He is a former contractor of NAWASA for the pipelines. He left all of us in Masbate, then his cousins stole copper which they sold to the junkshop; they were caught and her father was removed from work...he was desperate. We can no longer feed Joyce, our youngest.]

"Mabait ba 'yong nakabuntis kay Joyce?" [Is the man who got

Joyce pregnant a good person?]

"Naku, nambubugbog po palagi! Sinasapak po ako sa mukha tapos sinasakal. Nanununtok minsan sa panga. Kahit 'yong bata hawakan dito. Tapos sa isang balikat ihagis sa duyan. Binibitin n'ya to eh 3 months pa lang. Hinawakan n'ya sa pigi. Tapos binabagsak n'ya." [He always beats me up. He hits me on the face then strangles me. Sometimes, he hits me on the jaw. He holds the child here on the arm, then with his other shoulder, throws the child into the crib. He was hanging the baby when he was still 3 months old. He was holding him on the buttocks, then he would drop him.]

I was shocked with such a devious character. If he can do that to an innocent helpless child, he can surely do other atrocious crimes. No wonder he is now in jail.

"Ang cute pa naman ng bata." [The child is cute.] I affirmed the young madonna and child.

The Brokenness of Joyce

I asked myself what care can a baby have when its mother needs care herself? Her unformed breasts contain no milk to feed her sickly baby. "Nemo dat quod non habet," (You cannot give what you don't have) as the Latin adage goes. She was supposed to be playing hoola-hoop with playmates and peers in the streets, but she prefers to stay home all day. Joy is tired of going to school. She tends to be socially isolated and sequestered. She was violated and literally robbed of her youth.

This stigma of early pregnancy is also part of a cycle of poverty. It is mainly in poor families where you have very young mothers. In urban slums and rural areas, parents will not invest in the education of their daughters because they see them as liabilities. Girls will leave them eventually. Sometimes, the poverty also pushes parents to marry off their daughters as early as possible. Young girls in the squatters' area are much more vulnerable because they are practically powerless. Some of the problems these young mothers face deal with biology. Sexual intercourse, pregnancy and childbirth all carry risks for these young girls because their bodies aren't quite prepared for the physiological stress. There are all kinds of complications accompanying pregnancy, including a prolapse of the uterus. Babies born to young girls are often premature and sometimes stillborn. In the case of incest, the baby faces an increased risk of birth defects.

A question has been looming in the background of all these—a series of questions really, colliding and agitating each other like thunderheads in a summer sky. If this is God's world, why is it such a mess? And why do so few people experience good things in the way God supposedly intended?

Obviously, a great rift has opened up between the ideal world Christians describe as God's creation and the world we actually inhabit. We stand at the edge of a precipice and peer into a fog for guidance, and suddenly we have scars, scars that cannot be erased sometimes in a lifetime.

The brokenness of Joyce is not a simple but of a complex nature, for it includes physical, psychological, and emotional woundedness. It involves a deep feeling of low esteem and torture inflicted by an adult who was expectedly a caregiver or a hero for that matter. Protection is a foreign word. Child safety is just an illusion. The deepest desire of each of us in a broken world is to become what we were created to be: WHOLE.

I can identify myself with Joyce in her brokenness. God knows the gamut of emotions I have gone through and continue to go through.

"...hilumin mo aking sugatang puso." (...heal my broken heart.)

The best thing that can happen to a child like Joyce is that she be allowed to be a child still, even though she has a child of her own. She'll need help raising her baby so she can go to school, play with friends and have some chance at recapturing her childhood. God looks at each of us as His precious children no matter how stained we are. Nothing hurts more than a broken heart. Suddenly you feel alone and isolated. You search for answers but it seems there are none.

> *"The Lord is close to the broken-hearted and saves those who are crushed in spirit."*
>
> PSALM 34:18

> *"He heals the brokenhearted and binds up their wounds."*
>
> PSALM 147:3

Fully known, fully loved

I revere so much my late mentor and friend Fr. Chito Dajao. He was a seasoned painter and he introduced me to the arts. He inspired me and ushered me to the religious art genré. When I met a major accident in football many years ago, he spent for my hospitalization by selling a few of his works even if I barely knew him then. In my idle moments while convalescing, he gave me a sketchbook and a pencil. Envisioning a promising artist in me, he supplied me with tons of art books and supported me with whatever art materials I needed. I sensed that he was obviously doing this special favor in order to hone me and to utilize me as his assistant in his studio works or to be an added artist his congregation could have and use in the future.

I had other plans. In the course of my art training, I decided to ask permission from our superiors if I could leave the religious life and my resignation was approved a few months after. It was supposed to be a confidential matter. All these speculations about his motives on my future in painting would never materialize. I knew he would be frustrated when I broke the news. I haltingly revealed to him this secret about my departure, a secret I first disclosed to him. I prepared to return all the boxes of art stuff since all his plans were no longer relevant. "Why will you return them?" He asked sincerely. "They are yours and I gave them to you not because you are a member of our society but because you are a friend." True enough, Fr. Chito had been a real benevolent friend who guided me in my life till his death a few years ago. Art had been his legacy to me and I feel he beams with pride whenever I finish a beautiful work.

I learned from him a truth I would later understand about God: only if you are fully known can you be fully loved. My spiritual growth has meant bringing a succession of secrets, in fear and trembling, to God, only to find that God of course knew the secret all along, and loved me anyhow. I have learned that God is hardly surprised by my failure. Knowing me better than I know myself, God expects failure from me. I am more sinful than I ever imagined—and also more loved by God.

"Adam, where are you?" God called out in the garden. It was Adam, not God who hid. God takes the initiative to come searching; we are the ones who hide. And Jesus, the Great Physician, sees our sins not as disqualifiers but as reason for his journey from another world to ours. It is a reason for him to get closer to us. Rescue is God's business.

Fr. Chito told me that when he was in the confessional box, he would realize at that moment that the penitent is closer to God than he is. King David knew well what God most desires from us: "You do not delight in sacrifice, or if I will bring it; you do not take pleasure in burnt offerings. The sacrifices of God are a broken spirit; a broken and contrite heart, O God, you will not despise."

In childhood I thought of my sins as a brick filling in a space that walled me off from God. My guilt feelings blinded me to the truth that I was busily constructing a wall God had already destroyed. I now believe that God accompanies me at each stage of my struggle, present with me even as I flee from Him. At the moment I am most aware of my own inadequacy. At that moment, I am probably closest to God.

My children are closer to their mom. I know and accept this fact because my wife is an exemplary partner and a very responsible mother at that. She takes care of all the needs of my kids, from bathing, dressing up, and feeding them with good food. She teaches them and assists them in their homework painstakingly. She is systematic in her tasks. She's alert and snappily graceful in the house chores. I should say she is an expert mom. No wonder my kids are all drawn to her. All of them want to be near her side. *"Nanay"* (Mother) is the most oft-repeated word in our household day in and day out.

Absorbing the Mess

Our children are like tiny birds that flock around the mother's nest. However, when I hear the word *"Tatay,"* (Father) a spark immediately lightens up my face. Fortunately or unfortunately, it is a word associated with the toilet. "Tatay, I'm done. Pleeeeaaasssse wipe my butt!" "Tatay, I urinated on my shorts." I hear it when my little kids would call me after they moved their poops or when I needed to change their piss-soaked pants. It is my role in the house. As I flush the bowel with a smile, it becomes a magical moment for me. In truth, that role isn't my favorite thing to do with my babies. Cleaning them up is just my excuse to HOLD them. It is a chance for them to be near me. Absorbing the mess is just part of the process of getting close. That is exactly the same story with GOD.

Psalm 139 shows us that we have a God who knows all things. It is clearly understood from the language of the psalmist. It is most explicit in his description of God's knowledge of his own life. Listen again to the words of the psalmist:

"O Lord, Thou hast searched me and known me.
Thou dost know when I sit down and when I rise up;
Thou dost understand my thought from afar.

Thou dost scrutinize my path and my lying down,
And art intimately acquainted with all my ways.
Even before there is a word on my tongue,
Behold, O Lord, Thou dost know it all."

Hear the preciseness and cadence of the detail. Hear the exactness of God's knowledge. God's knowledge of you is so precise that He knows the words on your tongue even before you place it there. We have a God who cares enough about our life and knows the details of our life.

Norman Sustigier, a former Fine Arts Professor at UP and my great dear friend has taught me a valuable technique in painting called glazing. He uses it for his commissioned works for the Cojuanco and Ortigas families. It was also used by so many artists of the past especially during the time of Da Vinci and until the Renaissance period when Rembrandt emerged at his finest.

It is an old fashioned practice seldom used nowadays because it is quite painstaking. It is a long process and it takes utmost discipline and patience. The idea is to make an underpainting on every work. It means that you have to paint initially in monochrome. No colors yet except white and yellow. It seems lifeless and plain. The advantage and beauty lie when you put thin layers of colors. That's what you call glazing. In this approach, the painter does the painting two times, one in monochrome, and the other in colored paint. The translucent effect takes place even in dimly lit interiors. It glows. The highlights are more pronounced and the metals look like real. As a whole, the underpainting is not covered at all. Its strong effect gives light and life to the whole masterpiece especially on flesh tones. Most importantly, this technique makes the artwork last for hundreds of years because of the layering.

God builds up colors on our monochromatic past. Our live's underpainting may be lifeless and dry. He puts the color of his enduring love and compassion. He dwells in us. Here we see what compassion means. It is not a bending toward the underprivileged from a privileged position; it is not a reaching out from on high to those who are less fortunate below; it is not a gesture of sympathy or pity for those who fail to make it in the upward pull. On the contrary, compassion means going directly to those people and places where suffering is most acute and building a home there. God merges His colors in us and inextricably intertwines us to Him. Like the canvas of a glazed oil paint, we stand the tests of time. It is in the gloomy layer of our underpainting that His grace works all the more in order for our Savior to restore beauty to His marvelous creation in us.

I could not take my eyes away from the figure of Joyce. I felt drawn by the scar on her face due to her dumb stare. There are undoubtedly inner scars from painful events she experienced that did not leave visible marks, yet because of the visible scars, she remembers those events. She will soon find her healing. This live model of the Hapag has revealed to me the deepest yearnings of my heart. The yearning for wholeness. This is definitely brought to consciousness by the Hapag. This yearning grows deeper and stronger, thus making Joyce herself a faithful companion in my journey to wholeness.

THEY HAVE JESUS

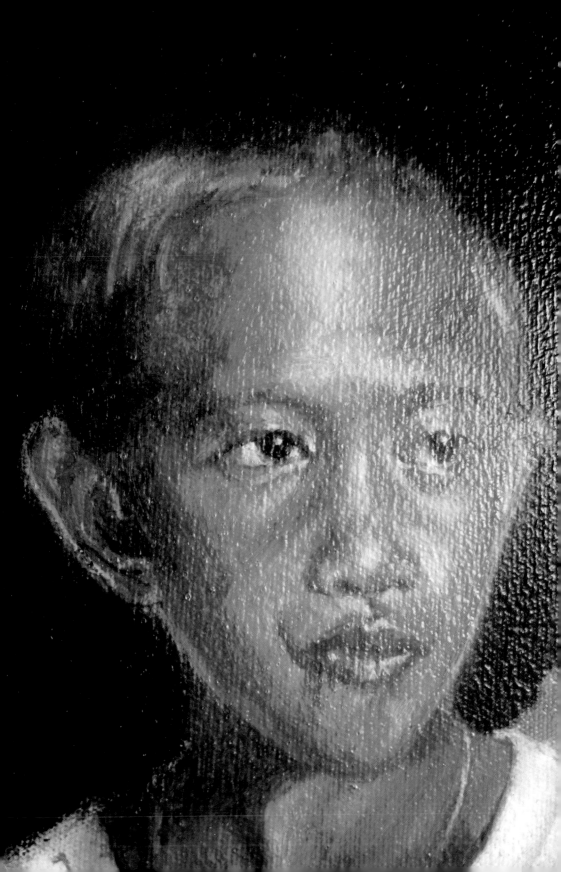

THEY HAVE JESUS

CHAPTER 12

The Far Gaze of Buknoy

B uknoy is seven years old but his face is the face of a weary forty-year-old bread winner. In the painting, he was the one looking far away and beyond, as if afraid of a danger that imminently lurks ahead. The fear of the unknown and uncertain future. This reference-model is anxious of tomorrow.

"After this meal, may we expect another one tomorrow? How about the day after tomorrow? Is there a future that awaits us?" Food insecurity threatens health at all stages of life, but particularly in early childhood when the critical growth occurs. Hunger threatens the poor kid

who has no sure source of nutrition.

When I saw him again after a year, I curiously inquired how he was able to pose so naturally. I asked why he looked pensive and if he remembered why his face was angled towards a certain direction. He recalled that moment very well. That was in the late afternoon towards twilight. He had a far gaze because in real life, his father is across the street at their doorway fuming in anger and waiting for the supply of food that Buknoy is assigned to bring home that night. He knew that he will get a beating from his cruel father afterwards. It was the very time we were having the photo session for Hapag.

"Papaluin po kasi ako ng tambo sa katawan ng papa ko 'pag wala akong dalang gabe at bigas at 'pag nalamang nakipag "picnic" ako imbes na nagtrabaho." [Papa would beat my body with the broom if I don't have taro and rice with me and when he finds out I joined a picnic instead of having worked.]

I felt so guilty for having taken his time and having pulled him unintentionally from their household responsibility and work schedule.
"Naku, sorry. Napalo ka ba nu'n?" [Oh, sorry. Were you spanked by your father the last time we met?]

"Nakatakas po ako. Tumakbo ako. Di po n'ya 'ko mahabol. Di nga po ako sa amin natulog nu'n eh." [I escaped. I ran. He couldn't catch me. I didn't sleep in our house that time.]

"Napano 'yong dalawang malaking peklat mo sa ulo?Pinalo rin ba ng papa mo?" [What happened to your two scars on the head? Did he

also hit you there?]

"Binuhusan po ng tubig na mainit ng kuya ko." [My older brother poured hot water over my head.]

"Bakit?" [Why?]

"Ginalaw ko po kasi 'yong side car n'ya ng walang paalam." [I used his side car without his permission.]

A wound within me throbs. It was a sight eternally etched into my nightmares. Buknoy is a malnourished dehydrated boy of the streets. Abandoned and neglected, his frail body is like a sheet of paper being blown by the wind to nowhere...joining odd jobs of selling sampaguita and begging for some money in the highway.

Instead of the sturdy legs that would have predestined him for the life of a wonder child athlete, he had, when he entered the world, totally inadequate extremities, quick to catch the eye, and touch the ready sympathy of the passerby. Since infancy, he rarely sucked milk. He was given coffee by his parents even as a baby. Through birth, or malnutrition, he had acquired a personality that could not be ignored, one which, at the same time, caught my interest and subtly disturbed me. There was something about him which differentiated him from the rest of the street children in Hapag for the notice of the tender-hearted. Where others bid eagerly for attention, and burst into voluble thanks and blessings, Buknoy sat silent, rapt in gloom. There was something deep about the intense introspection of his look. He never smiled, and he acknowledged my greeting only by a slow lifting of the eyes that had odd shadows in them. He was very small for his age and too old-looking for a child less than ten in age. His hands were unproportionately large and muscular, and, even when flexed idly in his lap, seemed shockingly formidable in contrast with his frail body. Unless you were unusually preoccupied at the moment of dropping a coin in his cup, you would notice that he carried away in return a very definite, yet somewhat disquieting, impression: a sense of infinite patience, and beneath it the vibration of unrealized, but terrific energy.

Buknoy best loved the late afternoons, when the street was quiet again, and he was already able to surrender the bounty, and the sunlight, deep with color, shot level over the low roof of the shanties to paint the faded lawanit and cooking oil tin sheets used as walls on the opposite dwelling a ruddy gold and turn the old rusts on the roof to burnished copper.

"Ano ang palayaw mo?" [What's your nickname?]

"Buknoy." [Buknoy.]

"Ilang taon ka na Buknoy?" [How old are you, Buknoy?]

"Ganyan po...." [demonstrates by counting and showing his fingers] *"Pito."* [Seven]

"Anung trabaho ng papa mo?" [What does your father do for a living?]

"Wala pong trabaho si papa. Si mama po iniwan na kami." [Like

this....seven. Papa has no job. Mama left us.]

"*Ilan kayong magkakapatid?*" [How many siblings do you have?)

"*Tatlo po kami.*" [We are three.]

"*Kilala mo ba 'yan?*" (I was pointing at Jesus in the Hapag Painting) [Do you know Him?]

"*Si Papa Jesus.*" [That's Papa Jesus.]

"*Ano ang gusto mong sabihin sa Kanya?*" [What would you like to say to Him?]

"*Marami pong salamat sa pagkain na binibigay N'yo sa 'kin*" [Thank You for the food You give me.]

"*Ano ang trabaho mo sa araw-araw?*" [What is your daily work?]

"*Nagtitinda po ng sampaguita. Namumulot din po kami ng mga lata, bote po sa inuman nu'ng mineral, pagminsan po nakakakuha kami ng wire na ang tawag ay tanso. Binebenta po namin tapos binibigay ko po sa tatay. Minsan nga po wala akong tubo eh. Walang natitira. Nasa tatay lahat. Gusto ko makatulong.*" [I sell sampaguita (local flower). We also collect cans, mineral water bottles, sometimes we are able to get wires called copper. We sell them, then I give the money to my father. Sometimes, I have no earning. Nothing is left. Everything is with my father. I want to be of help.]

"*Minsan ba may nagagalit sa inyo o pinagbibintangan kayong*

205

nagnanakaw?" [Are there people who scold you or accuse you of stealing their goods?]

"Nagpapaalam naman po kami 'pag may kukuhain sa may jeep eh. Tapos nagtatanong po kami. 'Kuya pwede pong mahingi 'yong mineral?' Tapos nagagalit sa amin dahil ninanakaw daw po namin 'yong jack." [We ask permission when we get something beside the jeep eh. Then, we ask. 'May we get the mineral (bottle)?' Then they get angry with us because they say we are stealing the jack.]

"Pero kinukuha mo rin?" [But do you actually get the jack?]

"Minsan po pero sinasauli ko din po." [Sometimes I get it, but I return it.]

" 'Yong takip nga po nu'ng lalagyan ng gasoline nakuha ko po tapos binigay ko po sa nag-jejeep." (I got the lid of the container of gasoline then I gave it to the driver of the jeep.)

"Minsan nakagawa ka na rin pala?" [So you were able to do it one time, or sometimes?]

"Opo .Minsan 'yong bote po." [Yes, sometimes. The bottle.]

"Ba't kailangan mong magtrabaho?" [Why do you need to work?]

"Para po makatulong kay tatay." [So I can help my father.]

"Masaya ka ba na kasama si Jesus sa picture?" [Are you happy that Jesus is in the picture with all of you?]

"Masaya po. Sabay kami kumakain." [Yes. I'm happy. We're all eating together.]

"Buknoy, masaya rin si Jesus na kasama ka." [Buknoy, Jesus is also happy you are with Him.]

Buknoy's cousin Jenny was 16 when she got married to a thirty-year-old man. She is childless but she manages to survive with a very small sari-sari store mounted on a street gutter. Soon, their place will

be demolished. She witnessed the hunger of the little boy but she could not extend fully her help because it was her husband who was financing that small enterprise.

"Naaawa nga po ako d'yan kay Buknoy. Minsan palaboy-laboy s'ya sa kalsada. Parang isang beses na lang s'ya kumakain sa isang araw." [I pity Buknoy, Sometimes,he just wanders on the street. It seems he only eats once a day.]

"Ano ang lagi n'yang kinakain?" [What does he always eat?]

"Wala po. Minsan may hawak s'ya sa kamay n'ya na isang dakot na kanin. Lalagyan lang po n'ya ng toyo 'yon. Minsan naman po nakiki-ta ko s'ya kumakain ng nilagang saging na saba." [Nothing. Sometimes, he holds a pinch of rice. He just puts soy sauce on it. Sometimes I see him eating a boiled banana.]

"Ba't di mo bigyan paminsan-minsan?" [Why don't you some-times give him food?]

"Binibigyan ko rin po. Kaya lang 'di ko maitodo dahil nahihiya ako sa asawa ko. Nakikisama lang kasi ako. Ayoko maging pabigat. 'Yon nga pong mga kapatid ko 'di ko rin talaga maasikaso nang husto." [I give him too. But I can't give him much because I don't want to burden my husband. I am dependent on him (her husband). I don't want to add responsibilities on his shoulders. I can't even take care of my siblings properly.]

Malnourishment

Buknoy's far gaze is characterized by deep hunger for food. He has no one to turn to. To sleep at night with an empty stomach and wake up the next morning with dry lips is a common thing for him. To find food or anything that would fill his emptiness no matter how unsanitary or unhealthy is always uncertain.

One apparent central aspect of the children's life situation is that they have been malnourished and abandoned. Sometimes the hunger is lasting, but more often it occurs for shorter or longer periods. Malnourishment is a critical situation for children of any age, but it is more difficult for younger children than for older ones. The consequences are, of course, a decrease in strength both physically and mentally. Not to mention, the disease and the effect on the immune system of the child which in earlier years seems to be stronger but gets weaker in later years.

Feed my sheep

In seizing the inspiration that came to me through Buknoy's hunger, I probed the important words of Jesus to Simon Peter the Rock when He said "Feed My Sheep." Three times Jesus asked Peter to reaffirm his love -- once for each time Peter had denied him. Three times Jesus reaffirms Peter's call to ministry. Jesus not only forgives Peter, he restores him fully to his confidence. Though this passage is an Apostolic commissioning, it hits me... my life is a tension of opposites on this regard. Reaffirmation and Denial. Reaffirmation in every time I feed the lambs of Jesus in the person of those who are in need, not only when it comes to physical hunger itself but in other forms of nourishment. Denial when I miss the chance of recognizing the face of Jesus in people especially those in need, and when opportunities slip past those moments when I could have done good.

I should say that I am amazed with the wonders the Hapag has done in my healing and transformative journey. It all started with a simple but aggressive desire to provide a visual reminder to my children. As I already mentioned earlier, my wife and I noticed early on that our little angels tended to be choosy with the food at table. At times, they could not finish what's on their plates. And worst of all, they would often ask us to bring them to the restaurant. Tired of reminding them every so often, I thought of this poignant painting which would show them a picture of hunger. It was intended for them to appreciate lola's food and count their blessings every day. Timely and providential, we had a big empty wall in our dining area which needed to be filled with a décor of still life or an appropriate last supper scene.

People who have been to our home have seen the original painting and the news for what they considered to be unique and original piece, spread like forest fire. The message was so clear: hunger. The call to action was even crystal clear: reach out. It gave me priceless joy that because of the many reproductions, not only my children and family benefited from Hapag, but other children and families as well.

Fr. Fidel Ma. Orendain, SDB composed a very beautiful prayer before meals that goes with the picture:

A FAMILY PRAYER BEFORE MEAL

Be present at our table, O Lord.
Our fellowship and food may You bless.
Give us strength for Your service.
In our comfort and peace
Make us mindful of those who have less.

Your children look upon with love.
The needy and those
who have nothing to eat.
Those older, but especially the small.
Let everyone grow in age and wisdom
In your presence and in the sight of all.
Amen.

In the question posed to Simon Peter on loving, feeding, and tending, I remember the query of my innocent godson in the States who was also named Peter. My kumpadre wrote me in his e-mail message:

"Peter is 8 and he asked: 'Are there real monsters in the Philippines?' I said no, these are not the ghosts or monsters you see on TV. These are real because day & night, children who are less fortunate experience these. I told him there are children around the world including the Philippines where they don't know where they're gonna get their food or if they're going to eat at all. They don't know where they will sleep, where they will stay, no toys to play with, no clothes or shoes to keep them warm, no grownups to take care of them. The monsters they encounter are hunger, fear, rejection, worry, coldness from the weather & COLDNESS FROM PEOPLE AROUND THEM. They are longing for somebody who will look after them and love them. Peter was so touched. But Peter is a

```
good boy. He never goes to sleep without
praying. He's got his Presence prayer book
tucked under his bed. My children are very
thankful to God for everything. They know
all good things come from Him and we put our
trust and faith in Jesus Christ His Son our
Lord and Savior. I am sure it will stay for
ever in the hearts and minds of the Filipinos
and maybe people around the world."
```

The Lord has truly blessed this work not only because it has sent me on a long spiritual adventure, but it has also reached the lives of people and urged them to help. The thought makes us pause awhile. It makes us rethink our loss of hope, loss of faith, and loss of trust in this sinful and confused world populated by us, the dispersed sheep who live lives as though there were no one to shepherd us, no one to herd us, no one to make of our unruly selves a unified flock. But this is exactly the image we are confronted with. This is exactly the "scandal" behind the promise of Christ: "I am the Good Shepherd." He takes up the cudgels for the lost, the least, the last, and the lowest. And He knows whereof He speaks. He has been there ... rejected, denounced, betrayed and even killed.

Concrete evidences of this were the billboards mounted on at least three areas in the Metropolis. Amidst the lures of fashion and the subliminal bombardment of brands and exuberant lifestyles along the busy avenue, the Hapag billboard took a pinch. It hurt and threatened, but it also gave voice to the voiceless who whimper in hunger in the dark of night. It suggests that the image we see portrayed in the painting is one of hope. It is hope because in the midst of an uncaring society, once more, we are reminded of the egregious fact that God cares. God loves. God haunts us insignificant creatures.

The tag line says: *"Do this in Memory of Me."* Another line follows at its bottom: *"If these Children are Forgotten, each day becomes their Last Supper."*

A passerby was almost hit by a vehicle because he was caught by the enlarged version. He once announced this to his community:

"A placard on EDSA Street in Manila confronts us with a provocative message!

Wishing that you experience and enjoy the friendship of Jesus."

"Do this in memory of Me" would mean feeding His sheep to pay tribute to a very loving Shepherd. *"Dining with Him"* meant, for me, walking step by step toward the One who awaits me and quietly whispers that He is not a distant God. He is a God near to us, sharing with us the sting of spoiled humanity: Emmanuel.

There were other charitable effects beyond my knowledge so they say, but I don't have the right or privilege to take pride in them, because I firmly believe that it was all God's handiwork and I was just a worthless conduit of his unconditional love and mercy. It was in reality, not my own painting. His Spirit breathed forth and His message just passed through my hands. Many anonymous benefactors have offered concrete help to the foundations which utilized it.

But beneath and beyond all that, I was startled with another aspect of feeding. Feeding not only means food for the body. It also means psychological and spiritual food. It would also mean belongingness. One of the ways to feed is to remove biases and provide a

213

sense of dignity to a person. It is holistic feeding.

A social worker once requested the release of a child at risk in the police station. He narrated an anecdote about the bully police officer who regularly sees the Hapag billboard in Makati on his way to the precinct. This man in uniform is notorious and known for his cruelty in treating street urchins. He claimed that he was held captivated with its timely message...

" *'Pag dumaraan po ako sa Pasong Tamo, nakikita ko po palagi 'yong malaking picture ng Last Supper na may mga bata. Walangya, kinikilabutan talaga ako. 'Pag nakakahuli po ako ng mga paslit, hindi ko na sila madagukan. 'Di mawala sa isip ko 'yong picture eh. Nakamarka.*" (When I pass Pasong Tamo, I always see the big picture of the Last Supper with the children. Gosh, I really get goosebumps. When I catch children, I don't hit them anymore. I can't take the picture off my mind. It's etched there.)

The food that the poor people need is kindness and DIGNITY.

Like Buknoy, I am restless and I always look far away. But Jesus invites me in a fellowship meal. With open arms, I know that Jesus wants to hold me in an eternal embrace. Seeing Buknoy again was a life-changing encounter. I imagine Jesus telling me: This is My Body. This is My Blood. I want to end this chapter with my adaptation of Verna Mae Thomas' Cross in my pocket. I thought it appropriate to entitle it "The Poor Kids in my Pocket" because the idea was to put the small Hapag picture inside the pocket and be reminded of our social awareness whenever we pick a coin or two.

POOR KIDS IN MY POCKET

I carry this picture in my pocket,
a simple reminder to me that
no matter where I am,
Jesus and the poor kids are always
in my midst.

This simple card is not a claim stub
to withdraw some blessings in return.
It is not a ticket to free me from guilt
nor a good luck charm to protect
me from harm.

It's not even to tag me as a man of charity
for all the world to see.
It's simply an understanding
between Jesus and me.

When I put my hand in my pocket
to bring out my wallet,
It is NOT for alms-giving.
This picture just makes me remember
that I must have a heart to share
that a part of me has to be offered
in simple service and deeds
to the countless little children
whose future is obscure,

215

who suffer and shiver in the dark;
whose voices are unheard;
whose nightmares come at daytime,
and whose monsters are real.

It's a symbol of my nearness to God.

So, I carry this little piece in my pocket,
reminding no one but me,
that I can give hope
if only I care.

THEY HAVE JESUS

EPILOGUE: Sketches of Hope

When the viewer looks at the picture, what thoughts come by?

When the reader looks at the thoughts, what pictures come in?

A year ago, I had little idea of how much I would have to live when I painted on that white canvas. I never knew that it would bring me to a long journey. I was just one of those struggling visual artists, finding a place under the sun while recuperating from an illness. I was just amazed at how an artwork could evolve from a mere sketch to a full-colored painting; from a monochromatic composition to a polychromatic imagery; from unilinear strokes to two-dimensional volume. The thrill of blocking, blending and smudging with bristle brush boarders on the technical and aesthetic. The different colors formed in unison: the shades of deepest blues, streaked with black, swirl and thrust out into pigmented relief, asserting a sensation akin to a spirit in turmoil and agony. This was the chroma of Hapag: Dark. Gloomy. Depressing. This was the color of my life. The evolution of my work led me to a real transformative journey.

I have always marveled at how an artist transforms an art piece. But I am more amazed at how the painting can transform its artist. I stand in awe before an artwork that has led me to a journey when I felt disturbed and I simply had to go back and immerse myself into the real stories of these kids. While knowing and discovering them have profoundly impacted my life, the greatest gift was the faith experience that enriched me in my encounter with them. Each figure evolved. They, too, embarked on a journey.

I was, at first, faced with the hard and seemingly impossible task of befriending them. A few of them were suspicious and hostile, but gradually, I experienced the warm, unpretentious reception of some of them who have nothing to boast about anything. They were the easiest to photograph. Poor children have little to lose when painted and interviewed. Without guile, they showed me who they were. I hope I was also able to unfold myself to them. Definitely there was hunger in them. But there was also a different hunger within me. I would rather have these poor kids' meal in order to dine with Jesus. I knew I had to pay a high price to be with Jesus. It is not a banquet where you stand tall. It is a meal where you lower down. It was not a question of posturing but a matter of how much I could stoop down so that the host could allow me to seat and stay near.

> *"The greatest among you will be your servant. For who-*
> *ever exalts himself will be humbled, and whoever humbles*
> *himself will be exalted."*
>
> Matthew 23:1-12

Slowly these kids were giving me something. These kids were healing something in me. I realized that it was a life-changing encounter.

The chapter pictures are detailed illustrations of each of the characters of Hapag. The deep hunger of Nene in the cemetery; the bruises and bondage of Itok; the simplicity and the warmth of Emong; the faith of the family of Jun and Roselle; the humbling experiences of Onse; the havoc of Tinay; the Sudan child in me; the powerlessness of Dodoy; the far gaze of Buknoy; the scarred life of Joyce; the wounds of Michael; and the friend in Jesus.

As a painting would have its own meaning to the looker or to the beholder, it is also true in this book. A poem can be interpreted in as many as the people who read it. Such is the same with this book. Even the meaning evolves; even the meaning and impressions are on a journey. While some have pitched in their interpretations of the painting, the readers are invited for a second look at *Hapag* in this writing. In any story, you tend to identify yourself. You find yourself mostly in one character, but sometimes in even more. In the process, you may also identify someone you know who fits the description. It may be the poor child near your place, a friend, a loved one, a village neighbor or even an enemy who needed healing and forgiveness. We ought not to focus on the twelve children alone actually. In your own context, who are these children? They might just be around. Hence, you begin to resonate; and in this sense, you begin to lead your own personal journey too.

At this stage, I am working on another SKETCH. This is about the same characters of Hapag gathering in a meal but using a different scene. The temperature of my canvas is sunny and myriads of bright whites and grey tones were washed all over it. It is a table of happy faces. The dilapidated table is fixed and refurbished. The chairs are neat monoblocs. They are all having fun and you can see the glow in their eyes. It is no sumptuous buffet but vegetables and fruits are served on top; bread and cereals abound. There are milk, chocolates and juice that they sip. They hold books and some toys. School bags hang around their shoulders and they are clad in neat children's apparel. They don't look like wealthy kids but they are surely healthy and strong. Their hands and feet are clean with no bruises and wounds on THAT NEW RESURRECTION MORNING. Shoes and functional slippers cover their feet. They are not lavish, but they just seem to have the basics of a happy life in the company of a smiling friend in the middle. At the background is a community where their parents build decent houses. They are not branded as squatters anymore. This is colorless though, but in this dream painting they have a chance for decency, dignity, and life.

This is just a rough linear sketch; a blue print so to say. These scribbles are for ALL of us to fill. It really depends on us and on our discretion what picture we would want to paint for these kids. The beauty of sketches is its unfinished character. How would we portray Jesus? How would we final coat these children? The answer would depend on us. The artist of hope in us is being invited to glaze and color such a black-and-white world. The final touches of how some figures would look like would depend on us and on how much we can afford to give or on how much we could actually afford to heal people. If in the reading of this book we find ourselves in one of the characters of Hapag, the sketches will allow us to paint the final picture which is the *Hapag-ibig* (Table of Love).

Time swiftly and hastily flies. In almost one year that I have not seen the kids, they have rapidly grown. Their situation has become worse by the day. Hence, it calls for urgency before it becomes too late. *Hapag-ibig* is a lofty dream painting. We can only do so much. Their journey out of the dumpsite will be a long and arduous one. Poverty is ingrained.

But at least, let us begin...to paint hope.

223

ACKNOWLEDGMENTS

This book would have remained just an idea without the gracious support of many people. I would like to extend my heartfelt gratitude to them.

My beloved wife Queeny and my wonderful children Marco, Chiara, Clarisse, and Marti. They give me reason to live...and to write. Thank you for loving me, for believing in me, for supporting me, and for bearing with me when I get too stressed up.

My dear mother Adelita Alvir Velasco, a guaranteed reader of this book even if everyone else would junk it or use it to kill flies. She will find every line predictable because she had whispered them to my ears when I was young.

My late father Ciriaco Relucio Velasco(+) who taught me perseverance.

My parents-in-law Felixberto and Remedios Suñga, who gave and entrusted to me their youngest child.

My brothers Jojo, Kuya Raymond and his wife Ate Sciony, my favorite niece Patricia. They hold a big part in my heart.

My brothers and sisters-in-law, nephews and nieces. Thanks for your support and care. To Kuya Edbert and charming wife Ate Ning for having consistently visited me in the hospital; Kuya Roy who gave me the idea to write a book; Kuya Dennis who revealed to me the secret of Ararat; Kuya Eric who gave me the book "A Third Look at Jesus," whose author became my dear friend; Kuya Ric for the use of his laptop; Kuya Atoy for his assistance.

To all my relatives and friends here and abroad. My cousin Ricky Feliciano of National Book Development Board and Ms. Asena Galang , for assisting me in publishing this book.

A feeling of gratitude is wholly appropriate when my theme is Jesus' unconditional love as I think of these my friends who work in God's vineyard. I feel at once enriched and undeserving.

THEY HAVE JESUS

His Emminence Gaudencio Cardinal Rosales, Fr. Chito Dajao, SDB (+) my mentor; Fr. Andrew Wong, SDB, Provincial (North); Fr. Julius Sanchez, SDB Provincial (South) Fr. Francis Gustilo, SDB, Provincial Emeritus and my "Kuya" who has supported me in many endeavors; Fr. Rene De Guzman, SDB who taught me English Grammar; Fr. Carlos Abesamis, SJ who showed me a new perspective on the Gospel truths; Fr. Louie Castaneda, SDB who inspired me in sincere acts of charity; Fr. Rafael DelaCruz, SDB who led me to the door of book writing; Fr. Stephen Placente, SDB who encouraged me to write my thoughts and who gave me some Biblical inputs; Fr. Jonil Lalap, SDB my brother and best friend; Fr. Chito Dimaranan, SDB for sharing me some ideas through email; Fr. Danny Loquiao and Fr. Boy Pablo, SDB for teaching me how to aim at my targets in life; Fr. Joey Paras, SDB who trained me to drink from the fountain of youth; my cousin Fr. Caloy Paglicawan, Rector of SASMA and Fr. Mimo Perez, the composer of the theme. Msgr. Romulo Rañada and Fr. Nonet Legaspi of the Diocese of Novaliches; The Society of St. Paul's for having disseminated my works in print.

Those who work directly with the poor: my great friend Mr.Tony Meloto who inspired me to make a difference in other people's lives; Fr. Rocky Evangelista, SDB of Tuloy Foundation, Inc., Bro. Elmer Rodriguez of the Ampon; Fr. Jun Bicomong, SDB of Ating Familia Foundation; Fr. Ronilo Javines, SDB of Pugad who gave the title "Hapag ng Pag-asa" to the painting; Fr. Boyet Concecion of the Emmaus Home for the Aged; Fr. Vic Robles of Bethlehem Orphanage, Fr. Egai De Jesus of the Dumagat Center Foundation; Manny Ortencio of Catholic Book Center and Adoption at a Distance; My spiritual Sisters Mother Mary Teresa Sideco, OCD, Sr. Fides Realubit, OCD, Sr. May Jose Racelis, OCD, Mother Mary Bernard, OCD, Sr. Cecile, Sr. Raquel Reodica, RVM, Sr. Gloria Ross, RVM, Sr. Bebet Gaston, Mr. Jeff Campos, and Ka Paco Dychangco.

Two years ago, I had a scary encounter with a masked man wielding a knife. I remember him with gratitude, though, since he was my nephrologist Dr. Genaro Yusi Sr. of Capitol Medical Center. He removed my left kidney which almost caused my death. The recovery period gave me a chance to study painting. In the same way I wish to thank my sister-in-law Dr. Edna Mallorca and Dr. Quintin Babaran who belong to the same hospital.

Most parts of this book were written in National Kidney Institute East Avenue Quezon City, where I was confined periodically and intermittently. I wish to thank the following persons who have offered me a warm and hospitable second home in NKI.

Dr.Gloria Crystal-Luna, Dr. Juat, Dr. Jennifer Balatian, Dr. Aisa Flavier, Dr.

Bacelonia, Dr. Urbis, Dr. Cai. The kind and beautiful nurses in the person of Ma'm Vicky, Ruby, Reah, Vic, Jary, Marie, Len, Lyn, Vans, Jamesiah.

My colleagues in the arts: Rona Chua, my friend and sister artist; Dr. Dan Lerma, M.D. a fellow artist, a doctor whose noble profession is as noble as he perceives the arts; Bro. Pancho Piano, who taught me some techniques in abstract art; Ka Fidel Sarmiento, our AAP President; Norman Sustiguer, a Christian who has thought me the principles of underpainting; My uncle Prof. Henry Alvir; Demetrio Delacruz, my best friend, who has taught me valuable techniques in the field of Arts and who designed the cover of this book; Ronald Ventura my idol and friend, Domeng Labordo who taught me water color techniques; Nemi Miranda and Abe Lucas my consultants; Eusebio A. Chua Jr. and Maximo Chan Jr. of Art Asia, who gave me the first break to exhibit my works in their gallery; Fil Dela Cruz and Cynthia Jamlang my cousin-in-law; Mr. Manny Duldulao and Ms. Marila Burgos.

I sent an early draft of the manuscript to a variety of my esteemed writers to get feedback, and the marked up manuscript I received convinced me that a relationship with God is as subjective and varied as the persons on the other end. I wish to thank Ms. Ilsa Reyes, Roy Mallorca, Bro. Drans Nolasco, SDB, Fr. Michael LaGuardia, SDB, Fr. Fidel Orendain, SDB, for their valuable responses. They helped me not only with the content but also the structure and overall concept of the book. In the early drafts I felt caught inside a maze; their shouted directions helped me find my way out.

Those who have enhanced the book with their comments Bernie Lopez, Mayor Manuel Melgazo of Leyte, Atty. Julio Gonong, Atty. Nick Acosta my neighbors and friends. My Batchmates in Tropang Busko '83 DB Manda; Kuya Kim Atienza, and Gabs Buluran.

Those who have helped in the printing process my Ninong David Lim and Ninang Leoning of the Iglesia ni Cristo, Tita Leonila Dayao, Andrew and Annie Lim, George Ta-ay, my secretary who transcribed the taped interviews, and Edward Gapas for mounting the manuscripts.

My driver Ner Mortiga and my assistant Judith Pelembergo for accompanying me in the areas of the Hapag kids.

To all these people I say a hearty "Salamat".

THEY HAVE JESUS

NOTES

1. The Niche of Nené

21. *"We rejoice"*: Romans 5: 3.
21. *Lahaye:* Tim Lahaye, *The Secret on Ararat,* 43.

2. Bruises of Itok

43. *"On a Starry Night"*: Vitaliano Dimaranan, 1982.
44. *"Eulogy: The Little Big Brave Man"*: Barcadios, 1993.

3. The Mosquito of Emong

64-65. *"There is an appointed time"*: Ecclesiastes 3:1.

4. Hapag of Jun and Roselle

76. *"Tanang ari-arian"*: Ricardo Ponce.
81. *"Take therefore no thought"* : Matthew 6:34.
82. *"A Worker will not"* : Matthew 10: 10.
84. *"You say 'today or tomorrow' "* : John 4: 13-15.

5. Jesus of the Slums

88-89. *"Hound of Heaven"*: Francis Thompson.
91. *"I have written"* : Isaiah 49: 16.
91-92. *"May your roots"* : Ephesians 3: 17-19.
92-93. *Abesamis:* Carlos H. Abesamis, *A Third Look at Jesus* (Claretian Publications 2000), 42-43.
94. *Yancey:* Philip Yancey, *What's so Amazing about Grace?* (Zondervan 1998), back cover.

6. The Hunger of Onse

105. *"If the rich person slips"*: Sirach 13: 22-23.
108-109. *"Little Flowers of St. Francis,"* translated *"Fioretti di San Francesco,"* 14th century books.
110. *"He was despised"*: Isaiah 53: 3.
111. *Albom:* Mitch Albom, *Tuesdays with Morrie* (Time Warner Paper backs 2003), 72.

7. Crawl Towards the Light

115. *"East Coker"*: T.S. Eliot, last part of no. 2 of 'Four Quartets'
116. *Augustine:* St. Augustine, The Confessions of St. Augustine (Garden City, N.Y. : Image / Doubleday, 1960), 335.
120. *"If Knowing the answers"*: Madame Jean Guyon.
121. *"God does all these"*: Job 33: 29.
127. *"Blessed is the man"*: Jeremiah 17:7.
128-129. *Mandela* : Nelson Mandela, *Long Walk to Freedom* (New York: Little, Brown), 495-496.
129. *de Chardin* : Teilhard de Chardin, *The Divine Milieu* (New York: Harper and Row, 1960), 86.
130. *Nouwen* : Henri Nouwen, *Making All Things New: An Invitation to the Spiritual Life* (San Francisco: Harper & Row, 1981), 51-53.

8. Fragrance of the Dumpsite

147. *"Nobel Peace Prize Acceptance Speech"*: Mother Teresa of Calcutta.

9. The Doll of Tinay

160. *Lewis* : C.S. Lewis, *The Problem of Pain* (Harper Collins Publishers).

10. Rumors of the Underworld

180. *"Strengthen the feeble"*: Isaiah 35: 3.
181. *"He gives strength"*: Isaiah 40: 29.

11. The Scars of Joyce

12. The Far Gaze of Buknoy

13. Epilogue

THEY HAVE JESUS

INDEX OF PHOTOGRAPHS

Joyce, detail of *"Hapag ng Pag-asa"* , Joey Velasco 2005 Oil on Canvas 48 x 96 in, *p. 183.*

Underpainting of *"Hapag ng Pag-asa"* , Joey Velasco 2005 Oil on Canvas 48 x 96 in, *p. 195.*

Buknoy, detail of *"Hapag ng Pag-asa"* , Joey Velasco 2005 Oil on Canvas 48 x 96 in, *p. 199.*

Sketches and study of *"Hapag ng Pag-ibig"* p*p. 217 & 219.*

FOUNDATIONS AND ORGANIZATIONS

Pondo ng Pinoy
Room 313 3/Flr. Pope Pius XII Catholic Center
1175 United Nations Avenue,Paco, Manila 1007
Tel.No.: 527-8113
Telefax: 527-8114
TrunkLine: 525-9126 loc.53

Ating Familia Foundation
441 San Pablo St.
San Juan Village
Chairman: Fr. Rolo Alcasid, SDB

Tuloy Foundation, Inc.
Tuloy sa Don Bosco Streetchildren Village
Alabang-Zapote Rd., cor. San Jose Village,
Alabang, Muntinlupa City 1770
Philippines
Phone Numbers: (63 2) 7750683, 7750484-5
Fax Number: (63 2) 7750483
Email: fr_rocky@yahoo.com

Don Bosco; Don Bosco Pugad
Home for the Streetchildren and Migrant Youth
Don Bosco Parish, Makati City
Tel no. +632 894 5932

Ampon ni Don Bosco
Don Bosco Technical Institute Makati
Manpower Skills Training Center
c/o Bro. Elmer C. Rodriguez, SDB
Technical Director
Pasong Tamo cor Don Bosco St.

Makati City
Tel No (02) 892 01 07 10
Tel/Fax: (02) 817 58 07

Don Bosco Boys' Home
Cotcot, Liloan
6002 Cebu
Contact person: Fr. Lamberto Paradiang Jr.
Tel. Nos.: (032) 4247002; (032) 424 7003

Don Bosco Youth Center
L. Flores Street, Pasil
6000 Cebu City
Contact Person: Fr. Donato Ofina
Tel. Nos.: (032) 261 0010; Fax: (032) 2620533

Don Bosco Boys' Home & Training Center
P.D. Montfort South, Dumangas
5006 Iloilo
Contact Person: Fr. Fernando Peralta
Tel. No: (033)361 -25-00

Don Bosco Boys' Town
Maa, Davao City
Contact Person: Fr. Genaro Taceban
Tel. No: (082) 244-0496

Gawad Kalinga
349 Ortigas Ave., East Greenhills,
Mandaluyong City, Philippines
+632-7270681 to 87 Local 47
Fax : +632-7231603

Bethlehem House of Bread

Little Baguio Baliwag, Bulacan
Tel. # (044) 766-4977

Casa Miani Fdn. Inc
St. Jerome Emiliani Road,
Sto. Niño, Lubao, Pamp.
Tel. # (045) 971-6263

PRO-LIFE PHILIPPINES FOUNDATION, INC.
Good Shepherd Compound, 1043 Aurora Blvd., Quezon City
Tel. # 421-9641
Fax # 422-8877; 421-7147

ANAWIM
#56 Chicago St., Cubao, Quezon City,
M.M., Philippines 1109.
(02) - 7258564